Caged Sparrow

Joseph Tuttolomondo
As told to Rosemarie Fitzsimmons

ISBN-13:978-1511923583

ISBN-10:151192358X

Cover designed by Anthony Cash

Special thanks to Jerry Fitzsimmons, Rebecca Glendenning, Michele Halbeisen, and Mary Graziano Scro for their editing assistance and insightful advice.

The Portrait Writer, LLC
Rosemarie Fitzsimmons
http://www.rosethestoryteller.com
rosefitz.portraitwriter@gmail.com

DEDICATION

To my wife, my daughter, and my son, each of whom suffered humiliation beyond what words can express and yet, they believed me, and in me.

Prologue

Attica
November 1977

People like me don't survive prison. I knew that going in. I accepted that one day, maybe in a week, maybe in six months, someone would probably find me lying face-down in an exercise yard with a shank sticking out of my gut.

They hated me that much.

I peered through the iron bars, straining to see as far as possible in either direction along the concrete catwalk, but saw no other inmates.

How many of them know me?

Considering Attica's population of nearly 2,000, the odds were good some of us had crossed paths, and they all knew I was here. I could only hope I'd see 'em coming and react quickly enough when the time came.

Truth be told, most of the inmates didn't know me, but they despised me just the same. Not because of my crime, though. Crime earned a man stature here. If I'd been a murderer, they'd actually fear me. If I'd been a thief, they'd give me their respect. If I'd been a drug dealer, they'd leave me alone. Instead, according to the inmates' unwritten code, I held a status lower than even the child molesters—those detestable scum who can expect to be beaten or maimed at the first opportunity.

I was a cop. And not just any cop, but an undercover narcotics officer and former chief of narcotics with the Erie County Sheriff's Department in Buffalo. They stripped *that* title from me the day I handed over my badge and guns. Now I was just Joseph Tuttolomondo, inmate number 77C633.

I'd spent the better part of 20 years sending drug users, pushers, and other criminals here to Attica and to other prisons throughout the state of New York.

My cold, musty cell offered no amenities, and not an inch of extra space. I could stand in the center and touch both walls. This would be my home for a few days while the state deliberated about what to do with me. I didn't have the greatest confidence in their decision-making abilities, considering that's what landed me here in the first place.

I'd given up asserting my innocence long ago. The boys at the District Attorney's office built a sound case against me, and I couldn't blame the judge for believing them. At my sentencing, when the judge asked if I had anything to say, I could only state the obvious:

"If you send me to prison you'll be sentencing me to my death."

"I know that," he'd said. "Maybe you'll meet up with someone there who couldn't bribe you on the outside and you'll get what you deserve."

I put my head down. No sense arguing with the Hanging Judge.

He sentenced me to "up-to-seven years" in a prison to be determined at a later date. That meant I wouldn't know the length of my sentence for at least a year, and that the state would have to evaluate my situation to determine which of New York's nearly 100 prisons would best suit my "needs."

Back at home, Audrey was probably just sitting down to lunch. *Would she be okay? Were there people with her?*

Hard to believe we said good-bye only yesterday. I'll never forget the image of her tiny hands in my large, shackled paws during those last moments. I'd tried to reassure her that I would be okay. She gave me a teary smile, but couldn't hide the worry on her sweet face. I entrusted her to family and friends, certain they would get her through this next period of our lives, however long it lasts.

Crossing my cell in one step, I gripped two of the cold iron bars, like the cliché hardened criminals I'd seen portrayed in the movies. Reality hit like a kick in the head. This was no movie.

I'm on their turf, living on their terms—a sparrow in a cage with two thousand cats.

Sure, I might not survive, but oddly enough, I wasn't afraid. I'd been at peace since that astonishing night I'd spent in the Buffalo jail nearly a year earlier. I knew I wasn't alone. Besides, I had street smarts. I knew the rules and I could play the game.

For instance, Protective Custody means nothing. For my own protection I couldn't leave my cell, but even sitting here next to the guard station I presented an easy target. If *they* wanted to get me, they would. An "accident" can happen in a split second in prison, and even if the other inmates didn't hurt me, they could make my time here miserable by tossing contraband into my cell and yelling for the guards. If I'm caught with something serious enough, it would mean a longer sentence.

I flopped onto the narrow bed just as the noon whistle announced time for chow, kicking off a rhythmic echo of gates opening and closing throughout the prison and inmates laughing and shouting to one another as they headed to the messhall. My cell sat conveniently at the end of the walkway between the regular prisoners and the messhall; they all had to pass me on their way to eat. My own food would be pushed through the bars later.

From my bed, as I sized up each man who walked past me, I became uneasily aware of the bigot I had been as a street cop. At one time I'd have grouped these men up according to appearance: large black men capable of snapping me in two, menacing looking Hispanics with anger and vengeance written on their faces, angry white men with black hearts, and Indians wearing hardened expressions of hatred and pride. The *old* me thought myself better than them, not because of their race (although that made labeling handy), but because they were losers. Criminals. Dope dealers. Addicts. Pimps. I'd felt only disdain for them, thinking, "good riddance" as I cuffed them. They could *rot* in prison for all I cared.

But now I felt an urge to stand and shout that I've changed. Apologize for the way I saw them...or refused to see them. Tell them I'd learned a lot since my arrest. No, it was better to say nothing. No sense starting a fight before I had to. Some of the men slowed to peer into my cell.

That one there looks familiar. Did I put him here?

"Hey!" A tall, heavily muscled black man stopped to stare through the bars. I sat rigid in the shadows, hoping he'd go away.

"Is that Tuttolomondo?"

"Who knows," someone replied, "Move on, I'm hungry."

The man shuffled forward, but looked back toward my cell until he rounded the next corner. I didn't recognize him, but I didn't have to. My arrival hadn't been a secret. When I'd walked through the doors the night before, they'd all been huddled around the television in the common area watching the 6 o'clock news. There I was on the big screen, larger than life—tough, hardened ex-police chief giving the media his last statement as a free man.

After the meal, the same inmate stopped at my cell on his way past, giving me a good, long stare. He nodded and walked away.

You'd better watch for that one, Tutt.

At supper time, the parade filed past again. I positioned myself in the cell's darkest back corner at the ready, awaiting his return.

He was in the first group to pass, but this time he didn't stop. Instead, his hand slipped quickly between the bars and flicked a small package into my cell. I pounced on it and raced to the toilet, certain I could flush it away before a guard arrived.

Something about the object stopped me in my tracks. It was just a page from a notebook, folded into quarters. I glanced up, but the man was long gone. It was a note.

Was it a threat? Is he trying to scare me?

I hesitated, curious now, and turned the paper over. Two words had been hastily scrawled on the outside in a child-like penmanship. I exhaled for the first time in what seemed like hours, wanting only to find this man and talk to him. I re-read the words, not knowing at the time that they signified the beginning of a most unusual journey—one that would change my life forever:

"Stay encouraged."

Omertà

1930s-1940s

Omertà.

It means, "Silence or death."

For a boy growing up in Buffalo's Little Italy, *omertà* was a way of life. Every Sicilian family on the West Side understood the code. You saw nothing. You heard nothing. You said nothing.

We knew all about The Family, called *the Black Hand,* or the Mafia to some. Once a respected organization in Italy that fought to protect family honor and justice, by the 1940s it had become a tarnished venue for organized crime.

My older brother, Caspar, first told me the story of how the Mafia got its name. I couldn't have been more than 8 or 9 years old, and I hung on his every word. According to lore, during the late 1800s, a young Sicilian couple's wedding plans were shattered when an officer from the occupying French army raped the bride-to-be, and she committed suicide from the shame. After the funeral, the grieving young groom stood on the church steps and shouted, "*Morte ala Francia, Italia Anella!*" (Death to the French, Italy Cries!) From these words came the acronym, MAFIA, and their battle cry.

The French officer was found and mutilated, and many Frenchmen were killed in the rioting that followed. The rebels then joined with Giuseppe Garibaldi and his Red Shirts to help liberate

Sicily. For many years after that, the organization helped local officials disband criminal activity; in return, officials would look the other way when certain activities fell outside the law. Power and greed soon devoured the group's noble roots. After World War I, its members began taking advantage of their own people, offering businesses protection "for a price" and terrorizing those who declined.

Many Sicilians came to the United States in the wave of post-war immigration, establishing settlements in the big cities like Buffalo. They brought with them their criminal ways, their "business" connections, and their code of *Omertà*.

Growing up in the shadow of *Omertà* turned out to be a good thing for a young man who would one day become a Buffalo policeman. I learned to be watchful at all times and I knew when to keep my mouth shut.

I have no recollections of our house on Erie Street, where we lived when I was born in 1931. My brothers told me it was a nice neighborhood on "The Hooks" along the Erie Canal, where it was not uncommon for the police to find a body floating after yet another murder had taken place.

My family moved to a three story house on Jersey Street when I was about four. That's where I grew up, and where my story begins. I loved our neighborhood. We could walk everywhere from my house—to the schools, to the shops, and to the church. In the summer, a green chestnut-tree canopy lined the streets, swaying and rustling in the Lake Erie breezes. In the winter, the streets were nearly impassable with snow. We'd bundle up under layers of outerwear to protect ourselves from the lake winds and have to scale enormous frozen mounds to get anywhere. We were a hearty crew, though; rarely did the snow keep us inside.

We lived on the first floor of our building. We rented the middle flat to a young couple and the top floor to an old Sicilian widow. I lived a predictable West-side life: every morning, milk was delivered; every holy day, we went to church; and nearly every day, someone was murdered.

When I was 5, the house across from Our Lady of Mount Carmel Church exploded in the middle of the night, killing five people. I don't remember the event, but I remember people arguing for years afterward over whether it was a gas leak, as the paper said, or a mob hit. Apparently, someone had been filming the event (a little detail that challengers found to be somewhat suspicious). My father would not talk about it, but the pile of bricks and rubble remained there for quite some time.

We didn't know specifically who was in The Family, but I learned later that many of my classmates at Grover Cleveland High were, or would soon become, members of Organized Crime like their fathers. I would even put a few of them in jail.

I became street-wise at an early age, developing a sixth sense about my surroundings. Sometimes I could just feel something was about to happen and I'd high-tail it out of there. Next thing you know, there'd be a shooting or a robbery. I learned to live cautiously, trusting no one outside my own family.

Our home, though, was a safe haven. My father, Salvatore Tuttolomondo, had a reputation as a strong and just man, well respected in the neighborhood. He did not belong to The Family, but he followed the code. Whenever anyone would talk about the *Black Hand*, I could sense his fear. He'd see someone get shot, or there'd be word someone had been hurt, and he'd put his finger to his lips and say, "We won't discuss it. Just be quiet."

Omertà.

Pa and his future bride came separately to America from Sicily, but they met soon after. Pa arrived in Buffalo with a wave of immigrants seeking manual labor in the local mills and factories, which were flourishing with the help of newly harnessed hydro-electric power from Niagara Falls.

He sailed into Ellis Island in 1905 aboard the *Napolitan Prince* from Palermo, and quickly found work with the railroad, laying rails and ties. He'd get on a train every morning, go to the end of the line, and work until sundown to earn another $1.35. It may not sound like much, but you could buy a lot with that in those days.

Ma came through Ellis Island also, sponsored by her brother, *Lo zio* (Uncle) Blase, a Buffalo shopkeeper. Before she came to America, her name was Katrina. An administrating official who processed her entry heard and wrote down "Katarina," which is

Katherine in English. She did not argue because she couldn't speak the language.

In accordance with Sicilian tradition, Pa asked *Lo zio* Blase for Ma's hand because he was her only family in America. They married soon after and had seven children. Pa learned just enough English to become a U.S. citizen. Ma learned even less. We spoke only Italian in the home.

Tuttolomondo means "all the world" in Italian. We embraced everything good from the Old Country: we were devout Catholics, we worked hard, and we were loyal to family above all else.

Ma took great pride in caring for her family, and she was such a fantastic cook that our home always smelled like a five-star restaurant. She was a big woman—obese actually, which contributed to her high blood pressure and shortness of breath, and made walking quite painful for her. But, like a typical Sicilian wife and mother, she dismissed these "inconveniences" and thought only of her family. She lived to serve others, and spent every day cleaning, cooking, and baking, just as she'd learned in Sicily—"I do by myself, then I know it's right."

Ma adored my father, and even after many years of marriage, she would stop what she was doing every evening to stand at the front window and watch him walk up the driveway as he returned from a long day's work. Her face would just beam.

"Ah, look how tall and how nice he walks," she'd say, and we'd all turn to watch him. What few English words she did know, she used to praise.

Pa read every word of *Il Corriere Italiano*—an Italian language newspaper that showcased Buffalo as the ideal destination for potential immigrants. Its stories painted the city as a land of plenty, where the American Dream was within reach for anyone who cared to work for it. Our real news, however, came from the radio. Every evening at 6 o'clock, the entire family gathered in the living room to listen to the local and national reports. One of us, usually the oldest, carefully translated every word. We knew we'd better get it right. If one of Pa's friends told it differently, we'd hear about it. He wanted the details about everything, except murders in the West Side.

I hated knowing that my father, a man of strength and goodness, had to worry about crime and live in fear of criminals. I think that's what made me decide later to join the police force. As a teenager, though, I thought the path ahead of me pointed only to college and medical school. Most of my family thought so as well.

Lo zio Blase owned a small grocery store across the street from our house. As hard as times were during the Depression, we could always count on him for a bit of candy now and then. Ma bought a few items from him, but much of our food, particularly in the winter, came from the lines of jars she stored up in the pantry during the summer. Ma was always preserving something: tomatoes, beans, fruit, whatever she could grow in our garden or barter from our neighbors. She even made sausage and cured it dry in the cellar. She fitted a nozzle over an old grinding machine to hold the casings. I had a big job when she made sausage. She'd feed the mixture into the casings and I'd stand by with a safety pin and poke air bubbles as they formed. I just loved to hear that pop!

Thanksgiving was always a particularly extravagant event in the Tuttolomondo household. Of course, being from the Old Country, Ma would never buy a dead turkey because you didn't know how he died. Instead, in the days leading up to Thanksgiving we'd have a live turkey tied to the radiator in our bathroom, right next to the commode. We had to push him away to sit down.

Just before the big day, we'd slaughter the tom and pull out its feathers, and then Ma would sear the pinfeathers off over the flame of our gas stove. On Thanksgiving morning, she'd get up at five to start cooking; there was always a great feast, with all the trimmings. *Lo zio* Blase would come, along with other relatives who lived in the area. It was truly a family event. Even all these years later, I can still picture all my brothers and sisters sitting around the table.

The oldest was Casper. He was much older than I, but I'll always remember him as a great guy who would do anything at any time for any one of us. Sam, the next oldest, was a hot-tempered perfectionist. Anger was his preferred means of communication, and because the rest of us rarely measured up to his standards, he often had reason to communicate. Still, his demanding ways paid off: he worked hard, and graduated Magna Cum laude from the university.

Then came the third Jenny. Two Jennys died before I was born. My parents just kept naming the girls Jenny until one survived. The third Jenny, my Jenny, she was special.

I loved Jenny, not just because she was my sister, but because she was my friend. We understood each other, and sometimes even communicated without words. Jenny had a mild, yet outwardly recognizable form of mental retardation. She also had a sweet temperament; she smiled perpetually and had a knack for making those around her smile as well. Ma made sure we were always nice to her, as if we had to be told.

Jenny made us laugh in her simplicity. I remember a day when my brother John (I'll tell you about him soon) came home once with some friends and they got on the subject of gonorrhea and Jenny said, "Oh, I get that all the time."

"I don't think you do, Jenny." John shifted uncomfortably.

"Yes I do." She grinned. "It makes me poop a lot."

We laughed because we loved her. We sheltered her as best we could from those who laughed at her for other reasons. I took care of her as much as I could. I still think of her as my sweetheart.

What I lacked from a big sister in Jenny was more than compensated for by my other sister, Josephine, who doted on me. In the summer, she'd take me on the ferry to Crystal Beach, an amusement park across Lake Erie in Canada. There we would ride the Cyclone and play carnival games for hours. If I close my eyes I can still smell those Belgian waffles and hear the live music from the dance hall.

Jo worked at Wies dress shop and got me a job there as a stock boy. She was in college by the time I turned 12, and her sorority met at our house. For some reason they let me stick around during the meetings. I guess they all thought I was cute. I remember listening to them sing and laugh for hours, enjoying myself immensely.

I loved all my siblings, but John, well, he was my hero. John had 5 years on me, though you wouldn't know it, we were so close. He was tough as nails and built like a bull. He was renowned in the community as a great wrestler, winning his high school division championship in his sophomore year, and I looked up to him. I rarely had to fight in school because everyone knew John was my big brother.

When someone needed a tree cut down, he and Pa would take off with big lumber saws to take care of it. They brought home giant logs, which they effortlessly split it into smaller pieces to use in our furnace. That's how John got into such good shape.

John and Jo were close in age, and attended socials together. Guys had to ask John for permission to dance with Jo. They respected and feared him, mostly because he would fight at the drop of a hat. John didn't graduate from high school, even though he was brilliant. He quit after his sophomore year and spent two years working in a low-wage construction job. I'll never understand why he did that.

Early morning on December 7, 1941, we were gathered around the radio when we heard the news that the Japanese had bombed Pearl Harbor. Not long after that, John was drafted into the Army. He saw combat in Europe, landing in La Harve, France and continuing on to fight in the Battle of the Bulge. He came home changed. He slept fitfully, reacted sharply to loud noises, and jumped at thunder. I tried to joke with him. "Whad-are ya, shell shocked?" Turns out he was. Today we call it Post Traumatic Stress.

I was the youngest, what Ma called a change-of-life baby. When she was carrying me, Ma became so concerned that I could be born with some form of malady that she prayed daily to Saint Joseph (as per Catholic custom) and promised that if I were born healthy she would not only name me after him but also celebrate the feast of Saint Joseph every year. Well, he came through for her, and Ma kept her promise. Every year you could tell Saint Joseph's Day was approaching weeks in advance by the zeal she'd put into cooking and baking and cleaning, until the house was brimming with delicious food and ready for visitors. When the day arrived, she'd open the doors to everyone, and beckon to anyone walking by to stop in for a full meal, as was the custom in the Old Country.

Religion shaped much of our family routine. Ma attended mass every week, said her Rosary every day, and taught us all to pray while we were quite young. She and Pa couldn't read the Bible, but Pa could recite High Mass in Latin. And of course, the holy days were a big deal. During the 40 days of Lent, we adhered to all the Catholic rituals. Among them, the most memorable was to visit and pray at seven area churches on Holy Thursday; we walked to each church, and they weren't all close. On Good Friday, from noon to 3 p.m., our home was perfectly silent while we mourned Jesus' suffering. The next day Ma went through the house banging on The Walls and shouting in Italian, "Leave us, Devil! Mary, Mother of God, come in!"

Every Sunday we went to church, usually at Holy Cross on 7th Street, where I received my first communion and confirmation. We children attended catechism classes there on Saturdays. If we acted up, even the slightest, word would get back home and we'd sure feel it on our hind ends. I went, of course, but religion wasn't for me.

I had trouble with church and all its rituals. Ring the bell, stand, kneel, sit, ring the bell again. I rarely paid attention, and when I did, I couldn't understand what was going on. Once, when I was taking communion, the priest dropped the wafer onto my shirt. I caught it in my hand and was going to pop it into my mouth, but he hissed, "Don't move!" Then he took it, put it back in the cup, grabbed a cloth, and mumbled something foreign before pulling it back out and putting it on my tongue. I was fascinated, but not impressed. I wondered what this guy would do against a gun in a dark alley. Mumbling and ritual weren't going to get him very far.

Naturally, I didn't let Ma know how I felt. Her poor heart wouldn't have been able to take it.

As it turned out, Ma's influence instilled in me a foundational respect for God, although it lay dormant for many years. If I'd truly understood what she knew, I could have saved myself a lot of trouble, but then again, I may not have had the opportunity to write this book.

Perhaps my favorite childhood church memory was Jenny's wedding day. Truthfully, we'd all been a little worried about what would happen to Jenny when we started leaving home. She certainly could not have made it on her own. One of Caspar's friends, Frank, took care of that for us. I don't remember exactly when he started coming over to visit Jenny more than Caspar, but we all knew for a long time that he was smitten. In true, Sicilian fashion, he asked for and received my father's permission to court her. Later, when it came time to ask her hand in marriage, he had to seek not only Pa's approval, but also that of all four of her brothers. Knowing how deeply she loved him, we granted it immediately. What a relief it was to stand in that church and share in their joy, and to know she would be okay.

By the summer of 1945, most of my siblings were grown and out on their own, and John was still in Europe. At 14, I was a typical teenager, looking forward to a long, lazy summer. I had no idea that the trajectory of my life was about to change.

It began when Pa received word that our beloved *Lo zio* Blase had been hospitalized. Pa told Ma her brother was sick, but didn't let on about the seriousness of his illness. Out of concern for her high blood pressure, we kept it a secret. Pa's plan was to wait until *Lo zio* Blase either got better or took a turn for the worse, at which time he'd tell Ma himself. For me, that meant sitting at home waiting for the phone to ring. My only job was to get to the phone before Ma. If the hospital called, I was to confirm his status without telling Ma, and then pass the word to Pa.

Like any typical teenager, I began to resent being inside. My friends were all outside enjoying the summer. Two weeks passed with no phone call. So, one afternoon when the guys stopped by on their way to play ball over on Porter Ave, I figured I'd probably be safe to take off for an hour or two. Of course, that's when the call came, while Ma was alone in the house making bread.

The hospital staff member on the phone spoke only English and had to work hard to make Ma understand that *Lo zio* Blase was near death. Ma removed her bread from the oven and raced up two flights of stairs with it to ask our Sicilian tenant to complete the baking. She told the woman there was still more in the oven and went back down to get it, but never returned.

One of my brothers found Ma lying unconscious on the kitchen floor. She had suffered a cerebral hemorrhage. They rushed her to the hospital, where she stayed in a coma for a month. To this day, I remember the remorse I felt when I learned what had happened. I've since come to realize that many factors contributed to that scenario, but there's something to be said for the resolve that is planted in your heart when you let someone down. I believe it gave me the tenacity to pursue difficult feats, and not back down when someone weaker depended on me. I believe it made me a better cop.

Throughout that next month, one of us had to be at the hospital with Ma at all times to interpret in case she awoke. If she came out of the coma, she would have been in a panic with nobody there to help her understand what was going on. So we stayed. My shift ran from about 3 p.m. until dinner, at which time one of my brothers would relieve me. Sometimes it helps to have a big family.

She came out of the coma, but was paralyzed and wheelchair-bound for the rest of her life. She'd experienced minor brain damage—nothing that would be noticeable to most people, but there were many things she could no longer do for herself. School had started again, and Grover Cleveland High was only 15 minutes away, so I'd high-tail it home every day as soon as school let out and stand by her side until bed time. I learned a lot about cooking in that time because she needed me to be her hands while she got dinner ready. She'd tell me what to do and I'd do it. I became quite the chef, and enjoy cooking to this day.

Ma wouldn't let her circumstances get to her, but treasured every moment. I asked about this one day and she told me a story about a dog trotting along the riverbank with a big ol' bone in his mouth. The dog stopped to look into the water, where he saw the reflection of another dog with a larger bone. So he dropped his bone to get the other and lost both.

"Be always content with what you've got, Joe," she said, patting my hand and beaming as if she had a great secret. "You've got so much."

That was a precarious year for the family, since we knew that any day Ma could have another hemorrhage and it could kill her. We tried to prepare ourselves for the call, but you're never really ready for that sort of thing. It came while I was in Physics class. I remember the phone on the wall ringing, and that I sensed something right away. I watched the teacher answer it, and he stared at me for the entire conversation. I said to myself, "Oh, no."

"Joe, you're wanted at the principal's office," he said. I looked down to avoid the pity in his eyes.

Casper and Sam were waiting for me in the office. They didn't have to tell me, but Casper did anyway.

"Mom died," was all he said.

So that was that. I was 16 and had lost my mother. It was the only time I ever saw my father cry.

I slid downhill a bit after that. My dreams of going to college and becoming a doctor faded, because now there was no money. Pa had no insurance, and all the money we could bring together went to pay Ma's doctor bills.

I helped a bit with my "weekend warrior" pay from serving in the National Guard. Yes, I was much too young to serve, but quite tall for my age, and I looked a lot older. I trained with New York's 174th Regiment on the weekends and conducted "maneuvers" one week each year at Camp Smith near Peekskill, about 30 miles north of New York City. On one of those nights I started smoking; my machine gun emplacement had become overrun by gnats, mosquitoes, and other "man-eating" bugs. That's when a wizened old sergeant tossed me a pack of cigarettes.

"Smoke these and you'll never have to worry about them buggers," he said.

It worked so well that the next night I came prepared with my own pack, and before that week was over I was hooked on a habit that would rule over me for many years.

Without college before me, I let my grades slide. I graduated high school, barely, and with little ambition to go further. Truthfully, I was relieved not to go to college. I'd always had trouble reading for more than 15 minutes because my eyes would start to water and the words would go out of focus. I convinced myself that I couldn't have handled it.

So, after graduation I headed off to the Air Force, where I gained some valuable technical skills. I left after only one tour and returned to Buffalo. John was home by then, using the GI Bill to get his high school diploma. Wouldn't you know, he discovered he rather enjoyed math and electronics. He became an electronic engineer and found work with Bell Aerosystems researching and developing guided missiles. I worked nearby at Sylvania Electric, developing radar systems for the Navy.

I joined John at Bell and we worked for a while in the same lab, developing guidance technology for the GAM-63 Rascal missile. Elsewhere at Bell that year, engineers were developing the X-2 Starbuster, a follow-on to the Bell X-1 Chuck Yeager flew when he broke the sound barrier.

Although I'd lucked onto a great vocation, doing work I enjoyed, I couldn't settle. Organized Crime was still rampant in our neighborhood and my father was still closing his eyes and ears to it. I kept thinking there was something I should be doing about that.

By 1956, I was making good money at that research lab. I'd also married, though not for the right reasons, and it didn't last. Still, that marriage made me a dad to Joey and Linda, two of the best kids you'd ever want to meet. I adored them both and spent as much time with them as possible. When little Joey started imitating his Daddy, I became so worried about him smoking one day that I quit on the spot. It must have worked because he doesn't smoke to this day. I wish I could say I quit for good, but I'd have to battle that giant again.

As a married man and new dad with a great R&D job, I thought I knew where my life was heading. Then I read an article in the newspaper about an upcoming police exam. Something in the article drew me in. I can't say whether it was the challenge, my growing distain for crime, or the look on my father's face when he heard bad news from the West Side. I took the test and passed with a rather high score. Before I knew it, I was called to go the academy.

First, I had to talk to my supervisor at Bell. At the lab I'd been making $13,000 a year, a handsome salary in those days. At the police department, I would be making $3,500 a year. My supervisor tried to talk me out of leaving, but I was adamant. He told me I was crazy and gave me a 6-month leave of absence to go figure it out for myself.

"You'll be back," He said.

Walking the Beat

1950s

I never went back.

During an intense six-week training course at the Buffalo Police Academy, I learned a lot about myself. First and foremost, I realized that despite the low pay, I was born to be a cop. I loved it all—the marksmanship training, self-defense classes, studying penal code and criminal procedures—I wanted the cop's life and everything that went with it. I poured through every text book and soaked up every bit of knowledge I could get my hands on. My eye strain bothered me somewhat during those late-night study sessions, but I would just read until the words became cloudy and then rest until I could see again.

Not only did I love police work, but I also seemed to have a knack for it that not all my classmates shared. I handled weapons well, scored high on written and practical tests, and I could rely on that *Omertà*-inspired sense of self-preservation to get me through some quick-thinking situations that disorientated some of my classmates.

Two training fundamentals hammered into my ethos during those short weeks mean as much to me today as they did the first time I heard them. The first is to maintain continuous situational awareness. When I went to prison, this principle prepared me to be ready for anything, but in law enforcement, situational awareness translates to handling weapons with discipline. As soon as I picked up a weapon, and before I could even think about taking a shot, I had to take in the entire picture: What's behind the target? Who's in the area? Where are all the weapons? I had to be ready at all times for an innocent person to walk onto the scene, lest I kill a bystander with a hasty shot. I tried to imagine how I'd act when the time came. How would I measure up in that split-second between drawing my gun and firing it? Could I fire if I had to? Would I remember to look for the innocents? I hoped never to find out, but deep-down, I knew the moment was inevitable.

The second fundamental I embraced was to maintain a high standard of honor and integrity.

"You represent the law," my instructors said. "Do not destroy public confidence by taking advantage of your position, accepting favors or bribes, or treating people with anything other than respect. You're there to serve them, not the other way around."

I considered the honorable origins of Little Italy's organized crime ring, and how easily power had corrupted an upright, decent family. I left the academy in 1956, vowing to be a good cop. I promised myself that, years later, when it came time to retire, I would still be able to hold my head high.

Like all rookies, I began my police career as a night patrolman downtown, walking the beat. My precinct had only two squad cars (one each for the East and West Side), so it was up to the foot patrol to keep the Queen City's residents safe.

By the mid-50s, Buffalo was changing in radical ways. For more than a century it had been the most prosperous city on the Great Lakes. Thanks to the Erie Canal, millions of dreamers circled Buffalo on their maps before setting out. It represented the Gateway to the West for pioneers, and the last stop on the Underground Railroad for runaway slaves bound for Canada. It also served as a beacon of hope and opportunity for immigrants lured to its thriving railroad, shipping, and steel mill industries. At its industrial and commercial apex in 1950, Buffalo's population topped 580,000.

The city's ports bustled with activity, and a line of stately grain elevators formed its waterfront skyline. Nearly all grain from the fertile Midwestern farmlands stopped here, awaiting delivery down the Erie Canal to New York City, making Buffalo the largest grain supplier in the world.

Buffalo's nickname referred to its prominence as the Queen City of the Great Lakes (Chicago being the king). Many preferred to call it the City of Lights because electric street lights debuted here, and the Niagara Falls hydroelectric plant brought power to millions. Frankly, I preferred its alternate nickname, the Nickel City, a tribute to the short-lived buffalo nickel.

Regardless of what we called it, by the end of the 1950s, Buffalo was a city in decline. The onset of aviation choked the railroad industry, and the newly opened St. Lawrence Seaway enabled larger ships to enter the Great Lakes carrying grain from the Midwest, thereby eliminating the need for Buffalo's port. Grain silos and steel plants closed, and "help wanted" signs disappeared. The once beautiful skyline crumbled as silos were torn down or left to decay, forming a feeble tribute to a great era. Amid such despair, only crime tends to thrive and prosper.

World War II also contributed to the change in Buffalo's character. Before the war, we all stayed in our neighborhoods: Little Italy on the West Side, the black population on the East Side, Jews to the north, and Irish to the south. Germans stayed in Kaisertown in the northeast, and the Polish settled on Kaisertown's eastern edge. A relatively large Iroquois Indian population, primarily from the Seneca tribes, lived wherever they could find refuge. Everyone respected each other's area. An Italian entering the German area was looking for a fight, as was an Irishman entering the Polish area. There were no other reasons to cross the lines.

However, the war created a true melting pot by bringing these populations together on the battlefield, where they defended each other like brothers. Combat friendships formed overseas carried into society back home, blurring some of the ethnic lines. As a society, we started inter-mingling and inter-marrying. On the one hand, this was good for the community culture. On the other, it enabled crime networks to expand and become more efficient.

In 1956, the crime rate was heaviest on the East Side. There we responded mostly to crimes of opportunity—robberies, muggings, domestic violence, and murders driven by passion. West Side crime, with its Mafia roots, tended to be more sophisticated, and consisted of smuggling, high-stake heists, and extortion. West Side murders usually turned out to be targeted assassinations.

I was an East Side cop, stationed at Precinct One in downtown Buffalo. I patrolled Michigan Ave and Eagle Street—Mitch & Eagle, we called it. That was a rough area, but I was confident, and cocky, and foolish.

Although I patrolled alone and we didn't yet have bullet-proof vests, I had protection. All officers were required to carry their guns at all times, even off duty. I carried a .38 Special, a beautiful pistol with a four-inch barrel. I also had a nightstick and a blackjack, which is a club with a leather-wrapped lead weight on the business end. The only thing the city purchased for me was the nightstick. I had to pay for my pistol, my blackjack, and even my uniform.

The squad car patrolled continuously. The officers in them would wave as they passed me and I'd wave back to say all was well. We didn't carry radios; we carried keys to the call boxes on the streets. If you got in trouble, you ran to the nearest box and hoped you could get the key into the slot and turned, and that relief could get to you before it was too late.

I worked 16-hour shifts, patrolling from midnight until 8 a.m., going home until 4 p.m., then returning to the streets from 4 p.m. until midnight. After that I'd get 24 hours off. Once each month, I'd get back-to-back 24-hour "weekends." Because I didn't have to report until midnight for my next shift, that amounted to five days off. It wasn't as glorious as it sounds. I used most of that time to catch up on sleep. I was usually so physically drained by the schedule that I was good for little else. What few hours I did have to spare usually went toward a second job as a security guard at Buffalo General Hospital that I'd taken to augment my low patrolman's salary.

This schedule and the demands of my jobs took a toll on my personal life. When the strain on our marriage became unbearable, my wife sued for a divorce. I didn't fight to stop her. I figured at the time I could be either a great cop or a great husband, but not both. It was not overly ugly, and despite our differences, she helped me maintain a good relationship with little Joey and Linda. I was somewhat grateful to be spared the task of telling Ma, because if she'd been alive it would have killed her...after she threw the Bible at me and dragged me to Holy Cross to plead with Saint Joseph for my salvation. Considering the situation at the time, I believed we were doing the right thing.

That's just what happens to police officers, Tutt.

Work kept my mind off the divorce. Patrolling never bored me, despite the routine and often uneventful shifts. I trained myself to keep alert, on edge, and be ready to respond at any moment. I broke up lots of fights and chased down more than a few muggers.

Arresting a would-be mugger presented some difficulties for a patrolman, particularly when it came time to transport him to the precinct for booking. On one occasion, while escorting two thugs (with their hands atop their heads) *and* their victim, who had agreed to come along to fill out a statement, I filed with my entourage past a wide-eyed woman leaving a dress shop. She immediately stepped back inside and put in an "officer needs help" call. Cops from every corner of the city came racing up the street—patrol cars, undercover cars, detectives, everybody. Despite my disappointment at missing out on whatever they were racing to, I didn't pause to watch, but marched my men toward the station. Then I realized they were racing toward me and became indignant, not to mention somewhat embarrassed. The show of force impressed me though. It felt good to know that kind of response was possible if I ever did need it.

Buffalo's bars closed around 3 a.m. Break-ins commonly began about an hour later. I checked a lot of locks on my rounds, what we called "shaking hands with doorknobs," first on the street, and then down the alleys at the back doors. I'd see fellow beat cops in the alleys in adjacent blocks, doing the same thing. (We recognized each other by our flat, octagon-shaped hats—who else would wear such a thing?) Occasionally our diligence paid off and we'd catch a burglary in progress. It felt good to know we made a difference.

I spent a lot of time outside White Tower, a 24-hour restaurant where business picked up after the bars closed. Derelicts would approach me in White Tower's parking lot and ask for a quarter. I wouldn't give them money, but I didn't mind bringing them inside for a 30-cent burger or a ten-cent cup of coffee. They often refused, because what they really wanted was to collect a dollar so they could buy a cheap bottle of wine or a six-pack of Iroquois Beer from the local brewery.

Sometimes, when the guys in the patrol car wanted to get a bite to eat, I'd sit in the car while they went into White Tower. I couldn't drive the thing, so I just sat there. If a call came over the radio, I'd run in, get the officers, and the three of us would race to the scene.

Business at White Tower picked up with the winter weather, particularly in January and February. That's when temperatures dipped into the teens, which, combined with the icy lake winds, could easily kill a man. The restaurant served as a safe haven for anyone who could scrounge a dime. Men and women would nurse a single cup of coffee for hours just to stay inside. However, anyone who wasn't buying had to leave. It wasn't uncommon for the truly destitute to approach me and say, "Hey, Tutt, can you get me 30 days?" I'd arrest them for vagrancy and then appear with them in court to say they were disrupting society. The judge knew what was up, so for 30 days or more, they'd sit in a cell, grateful for a warm bed and some hot food.

One would expect criminal activity to wane in the winter months, but regrettably, crime has no season. In January 1959, a particularly strong storm blew in from the lake. The massive drifts and high winds stranded more than 220 cars along Fuhrman Boulevard. We were all called to report for duty, and we spent much of the night pulling citizens from their vehicles. While we were digging people out, the looters were smashing windows all over town. There were four break-ins over on South Park Ave., mostly service stations, and others at a jewelry store on Broadway, a studio downtown, and three or four delicatessens.

Days like that were exceptions. More often than not, I just served as a reminder that the police were near should anyone either need help or be thinking about committing a crime.

In the early morning hours, I'd spend a lot of time sending drunks home. They weren't generally threatening, but drunks on the streets were prime mugging targets. That's how I met Scout. I was making my rounds past a restaurant bar near the corner of Mitch &

Swan that was a popular hangout for Indians. Buffalo's sizeable Indian population worked primarily as iron workers, constructing superstructures for bridges and buildings. When I saw Scout tumble out of the bar and onto the street, I remember thinking he was one of the largest men I'd ever seen.

I never learned his real name. His ancestors belonged to the great Seneca Nations who had lived in the region for centuries. They fought for the Americans in the War of 1812 and suffered heavy casualties. In return, America forced them onto reservations at Buffalo Creek and four other "convenient" locations. However, by 1850, most of the Indians had been kicked off that land as well, with the help of a handy document called the Indian Removal Act. Those Indians who didn't move west did their best to make a living in the settled cities, but many succumbed to the same alcoholic fate that killed their forefathers.

Scout's real name might have been a badge of honor. For all I knew, he could have been a descendent of Chief Red Jacket, Buffalo's great Seneca orator and negotiator, who was given the silver Peace Medal by George Washington himself. But I was ignorant to all this, and an insensitive cop, so I just called him Scout.

On this particular night, Scout was drunk out of his mind. I figured he lived in a nearby Indian boarding house, so we started walking in that direction. That is, I walked, struggling to hold up his giant frame, while he staggered and sang and giggled. I got him to the boarding house and handed him over to the guy who answered my knock and confirmed his residency. Before they went inside, I pulled Scout's head back by his greasy hair so I could look into his one open eye.

"Scout, if I see you on the street again like this, I'm going to lock you up."

He gave me a wide grin and passed out on the floor.

In my mind, I was one fine police officer. I had a knack for knowing where to be and how to respond, when to advance and when to back off. I could have arrested Scout, but he was a relatively harmless drunk and I knew drinking was one of the few pleasures he had.

With the exception of Scout, my years on the beat are a long-ago blur, and most of the people and places have faded from memory. However, I'll never forget Rocky's Place, a loud bar on the busy corner of Mitch & Eagle, nor the courage I sometimes had to muster just to walk past its doors.

As a patrol officer, I didn't go into Rocky's. We were told not to because we would never come out. Its patrons were all East Siders, and the criminal activity behind those doors was too nefarious for a rookie cop with only a pistol and a night stick for protection. I didn't know at the time, but later, when I became part of the narcotics division, we would learn exactly what was happening in there and I would get my chance to go in and clean it up.

Still, we did have to show a police presence in the area. It was common most nights, and particularly on a payday Friday, for a crowd of partiers in various stages of drunkenness to spill from the bar onto the sidewalks. We hoped that with regular patrols our presence would at least stem the most overt criminal activity.

I was still relatively new to the force when a patrol past Rocky's turned into an event I'll never forget. It was about 2 a.m., and Rocky's was hopping. The blaring music from the street made me wonder how anyone inside would possibly hear anything for the next week. There was the usual sidewalk activity and obvious drunken behavior that I did my best to ignore. I figured that if I waited down the street, I might be able to help some of them get home safely.

I walked past two men who probably should have quit drinking five beers earlier. The first man looked my uniform up and down, and a tooth-deprived grin crept across his face.

Aw, heck, here it comes.

"Looky here, Louie. Ain't he cute with all them little buttons?"

Louie snickered.

"Hey, mailman, where's my Gub'ment check?" Louie's breath was so foul I could swear I saw a green cloud form in front of him.

A warm rage crept up the back of my neck. I wanted to pull out the pistol—show 'em I wasn't afraid—but that would have been disastrous in such a crowd.

It's just words, Tutt. They're not breaking any laws.

I gripped my nightstick so tightly that the top dug into my wrist. I crossed in front of them, doing my best to ignore their litany of taunts and jeers. When I didn't rise to their bait, one of them shoved my shoulder as I tried to step past him. I'd known all along they just wanted to fight.

Ol' Louie came rushing at me, fists waving, head down in a ramming tilt; his buddy leapt on my back. I thrust the nightstick at Louie and he went down immediately, but I couldn't shake the sidekick. He wrapped around me like a wet sheet. I tried hitting him in the groin, smacking the stick over my shoulder, and slamming backward into the lamp post, but I couldn't get to him.

Then all of a sudden, he was gone. I figured I must have landed a punch in there somehow, which was odd, because I hadn't felt any impact.

Then I turned and there was Scout, holding the guy by the scruff of his neck and grinning like a kid who'd won a prize at the fair.

"Whad'ya want me to do with him?" He thrust his prize toward me for inspection.

"Well I guess you can give him to me. I'll just take these boys down to the station for a visit. Nice work, by the way."

I handcuffed both troublemakers, called for the car, and arrested them for assault on a police officer. I've long-since lost track of Scout, but I'll always be grateful that he'd been there that night.

Overall, patrolling was a good gig. I became accustomed to the rhythm of the city streets, and I liked knowing I was part of it. After four and a half years, though, I started yearning for more action—a little adventure. I knew the bad guys were operating all over this city, in places a beat cop wasn't likely to enter. I wanted a shot at shutting them down.

Right about that time, a couple of thugs pulled off a series of robberies against the employees of an East Side bakery. Most of the workers at this bakery were hardworking men of Polish descent who lived in homes nearby. They walked to work early each morning to get the kitchen open and start the bread for that day.

These two thugs had figured out the bakers' routine and began intercepting them regularly along the route, beating them and taking their money. The bakers stopped carrying money, but that didn't seem to matter; the attacks continued. I and a few other patrolmen tried beefing up our presence on the streets around the bakery in the early hours; it helped, but we didn't have the manpower to be everywhere at all times. As soon as we'd let up, it would happen again, or we'd be on one block and they'd show up on another.

Back at the precinct, my lieutenant told the watch that we'd have to go undercover to catch these thugs, and asked, "Who'd like to take a crack at that?" I jumped at the chance to do something exciting, and so did a fellow patrolman named Capardi. The two of us dressed up like derelicts, bought pints of cheap Thunderbird wine to stick in our back pockets, and sat ourselves down on the curb like a couple of drunks. Nothing happened for many days, except that our clothes became dirtier, our beards scragglier, and we eventually blended into the landscape.

We spent several nights outside that bakery; Capardi sat, half stooped over, on one curb and I sprawled on another across street. One evening, Capardi had to take the night off for something happening at home, so they assigned me another partner. We had to make him look bad in a hurry because the lieutenant didn't want me out there alone. Naturally, that night they struck, attacking the bakers right in front of us! One of them even stopped and looked at me as he took off. We jumped up, gave chase, and arrested them before they knew what hit 'em. Later at the station, one of the thugs being booked stared at me nonstop, shaking his head.

"I never woulda' figured you for a cop," he kept saying.

My first undercover bust; such adrenaline! I'd had a taste of walking on the edge, and enjoyed it immensely. It was pure ego; I'd pitted myself against some tough customers and come out on top; I figured I was pretty sharp. Sure, I'd always thought I was street-wise, but now I was also "cop-wise."

Returning to a walking beat after such an exciting taste of victory made my job seem crossing-guard tame. Now that I'd experienced undercover work, I'd never be content as a beat cop. I wanted Vice.

Undercover

1960s

I pounded the pavement for six long, restless months after that bakery gig. With every bust that went down in Vice without me, I became a little more determined to find a way in. They needed me, this I knew. What I didn't know, as the 1960s began to unfold, was that Buffalo was about to implode under the crushing pressures of political, cultural, and physical change, and that as a police officer, I'd have a front row seat from which to watch its destruction.

With the United States at war in Vietnam, many of Buffalo's youth allied with a national movement that vilified government as the real enemy. Students from the University at Buffalo organized rallies and sit-ins to protest the war, and the draft in particular.

Their protests grew progressively volatile throughout the decade, until August 1969, when a group of demonstrators took their message off campus and set up a station on Elmwood Avenue under the sanctuary of a West Side Unitarian Church. For 12 days they waved banners, held anti-government protest workshops, smoked marijuana openly, and delivered public anti-war tirades to passersby, attracting hundreds to the church grounds.

On August 19, Federal agents, U.S. Marshals, and Buffalo Police officers stormed the church and arrested nine demonstrators (who received notoriety as The Buffalo Nine), some of whom were military deserters. Through the next year, as the Nine were tried in court, protesters continued to rage against the war, against campus ROTC programs, and now against police officers and judges.

In October of 1969, just after two of the draft evaders received three-year sentences, more than 5,000 demonstrators marched from the campus to Niagara Square as part of the National Moratorium against the Vietnam War. By that time, most of the city had grown weary of student-led protests, so they didn't seem to mind when the Buffalo Police went in to break up the march.

On the cultural front at that time, the Hippie movement was encouraging people to drop out of school and go against "The Establishment." Marijuana and heroin use was on the rise, heavily romanticized in literature and in that newly popular Rock & Roll. It also became stylish to mock the traditional Judeo-Christian values and embrace Eastern cultures and philosophies.

The 60s were loud and violent times, during which Buffalo sustained substantial moral and social wounds. Some the hardest blows to the city, however, were physical.

Buffalo's urban topography had been designed in 1804 by surveyor Joseph Ellicott, who created a radial street plan based on Pierre L'enfant's layout of Washington, D.C. He laid out the city in a way that could sustain growth well into the 20th Century. Later, during the 1930s, the entire city blossomed as a canvas for art deco-style creativity, from the grandiose City Hall and Lafayette Hotel to the beautiful Buffalo Central Terminal. Renowned architects were drawn to Buffalo. Frank Lloyd Wright designed his first commercial office building here, the Larkin Soap Company, and artists like Daniel Burnham and Louis Henry Sullivan added their styles to Buffalo's flourishing industrial skyline. But it was all for naught.

By the late 60s, the Larkin building had been demolished and the others were falling into disrepair. In the name of Urban Renewal, giant swaths of Ellicott's controlled design were torn up and replaced with a haphazard collection of malls, high rises, and expressways. Many of the beautiful Victorian homes in Little Italy were swept away with the destruction, to make way for public housing projects.

In a sense, my past was unraveling, but my work kept pushing me forward. In 1962, a window of opportunity opened when I heard the Vice unit was looking for young men who could blend into a crowd. I was a perfect candidate. I looked young for my age and I had already proven myself in action. I was also single by then, unencumbered by daily family responsibilities, and could therefore commit to spending hours undercover. I applied for and received a transfer.

The unit's proper title was the Vice, Liquor and Gambling department. As soon as Captain Carson, head of the VLG, accepted my transfer request, he sent me through a training program to soak up everything I could about gambling, prostitution, card games, and moonshine. The course presented a rather sharp learning curve for me because I'd never participated in any of those pastimes.

Many of Buffalo's shadiest entrepreneurs in the 60s tried their hand at making and selling moonshine. Fortunately for us, moonshiners were not the brightest criminals. You could always spot them, particularly in the winter, because they'd build their stills in basements and put holes through the floors so they could run tubing up to the roof. Once they lit the fire, the snow melting off the roof was like a neon sign to law enforcement officers. However, every time we broke up an activity, the moonshiners seemed surprised that we found them.

Moonshining was small potatoes compared to some of the other criminal activity of the era. My primary area of responsibility was to quell homosexual activity (which was considered a crime at the time) and prostitution.

On one of my early calls, my partner and I responded to local post office workers' complaint about a group of homosexuals who were accosting them while they made their rounds. We walked the route with the workers, and as we neared the trouble area I hung back a bit, as if I were a loner. A man approached me almost immediately.

"Hey honey," he said, "you want to have a good time?"

He was a small man, in his early 20s, dressed in a t-shirt and jeans. His smile, however, was anything but ordinary; it bordered on maniacal and made my spine tingle. This was a bad man. I had to remind myself that I turn toward trouble for a living. I said, "Sure, what are we going to do?"

He invited me into a nearby apartment and I followed. My partner waited outside to let me handle the bust. No sense blowing his cover if he didn't have to. We started up a flight of stairs while the suspect told me what he was going to do and said he required no payment. That was all I needed to hear, so I stopped right there in the stairwell and got as far as, "Mister, I'm placing you under arrest for—" when another man, clearly his associate, appeared from nowhere and tackled me. Oh wow, was this guy strong! They both started grappling with me, trying to throw me down the stairs. I grabbed one guy by the hair, which turned out to be a wig and it came off in my hands! He took off running, but by that time my partner arrived on the scene and we arrested both men.

I had no pity on the people I arrested. They were scum, as far as I was concerned and deserved to be put away. That's what I thought about the derelict reportedly hanging around the public restroom at a downtown park offering young men drugs for sexual favors.

Dressed like an aimless 20-something, I sauntered down to the park with a stack of comic books and sat on a bench near the restrooms. My partner sat in an unmarked car in a nearby parking lot. On the second day of my vigil, the perpetrator approached me. I have to say, I hadn't expected someone wearing a suit and tie.

He offered me some "downers" if I'd let him take me into one of the stalls.

Scumbag.

As soon as I agreed, he handed over a fist full of pills.

"You can have the rest when we finish." He gave the area a furtive glance, then hustled me forward. The moment he touched the restroom door, I identified myself, signaling to my cover man to come assist with the arrest.

"NO! You can't!" The man started melting down before my eyes. "I'm a professor at a school for gifted children…this will ruin me!"

"Well, now, ain't that tough?" I despised him more for this revelation. I signaled my partner, and he started heading toward us.

"Wait, wait." The man lowered his voice. "You should know, I'm a man with many influential connections…I can make your life miserable if you don't drop this. Tell your partner this was a mistake."

I looked him square in the eyes.

"Don't even *think* of trying to dodge this. I'll be watching your case. If you don't do time, I'm going to blow this wide open in the news media. At any rate, you're not going back to that school."

By the time we arrived at the station, he was a beaten man.

Arrests like that one were rare, however. I spent the bulk of my undercover days rubbing elbows with pimps and call girls. The two primary types of crime committed in this line of work are the prostitution itself, and robbery. Sometimes "customers" were robbed by the prostitutes; other times they were simply lured by the promise of sex, but were rolled instead. I spent many hours on the street dressed up like someone smart enough to earn some pocket money, but gullible enough to need help spending it. Legally, I could only make an arrest if I witnessed an overt act that would fulfill the requirements of a crime; this meant a prostitute had to actually take money and begin disrobing.

I made more than 200 arrests in one year, primarily high-class call girls. As a result, I was promoted from acting detective to full detective in 1963. I started smoking again, cigars this time, which I inhaled like cigarettes. Not only did they suit my undercover persona, but they also seemed to cut the tension during our more stressful missions.

I can't say I enjoyed my work. At times it was downright depressing to meet so many depraved people, but I knew I was good at my job and that my efforts helped make a difference.

Every once in a while, I'd get a case that just seemed to make less sense than all the others. I'll never shake the memory of Melinda, a lovely girl whose husband was a banker. She had everything. If all she wanted was to cheat on her husband, she could have easily found someone else. But she was charging people, and we got a complaint, so I nabbed her. Her trial went on for a long time. I felt sorry for her poor husband, an upright citizen, straight as an arrow; his devastated face made good front-page fodder for the local papers. I don't remember whether she was acquitted or if she was given probation, or perhaps the charges were dropped, but I do know that when the trial ended, she and her husband left town. I lost track of her after that, but I still mourn for what she gave up. To me, Melinda epitomized what was and still is wrong with this nation's youth: they undervalue their self-worth, and settle for being something far less than they might become.

Like most police officers, I worked a second job to augment my meager $3,500 salary. Since 1958, I'd been a security officer at Buffalo General Hospital, which was located in a neighborhood that had become caught up in the city's blight. The hospital's dimly lit parking lots were ideal for purse snatchers and perverts. I patrolled outside, particularly during the 11 p.m. shift change, to help nurses reach their cars safely.

I met a pretty nurse there named Audrey, who was different from the other women I knew. There was a peace about her that I liked very much. Of course, considering my recent divorce, I had no plans to start a relationship, but her serenity drew me in and I found numerous reasons to be on her floor when she was on duty and in the parking lot when she left.

One evening, I was leaning against the nurse's station reception desk chatting with Audrey while we waited for the on-coming shift to arrive. A nurse named Ginny stormed in, muttering.

"The old creep! I could just scream." She flung her parka and scarf onto the coat rack and turned toward us, her cheeks crimson.

"Is he out there again?" Audrey rose and motioned for me to follow. She stopped at the water cooler and filled a paper cup, which she took to Ginny. "I thought that was a one-time thing."

"No, this is the third time this week—my first, but he flashed Nicole last night on Ellicott Street and Kay in the High Street lot Saturday night." Ginny took the cup and downed its contents. "He's decided to stay, I'm afraid."

I yanked out my notepad.

"Not on my turf, he won't." I flipped to an open page. "Tell me about this jerk."

The girls gave me a detailed description of the flasher, an older man in a dark trench coat. He seemed to have no established pattern for where and when he "revealed" himself. I stood watch in the parking lot that night, and even walked around the hospital twice, but saw nothing suspicious.

Not a problem. I've got plenty of time.

The man struck again the next night on High Street while I patrolled Ellicott, and then he appeared in the front parking lot as I staked out the back. This went on for weeks; he always showed up on a street where I wasn't. I thought perhaps he was watching for me, so for a few nights I actually hid under cars, hoping he'd think the coast was clear, but to no avail.

I went up to the psych ward and spoke to a doctor there to see if I could figure out how this guy's mind worked; he told me a lot about psychotic behavior, but nothing that would help me catch a pervert.

One evening, as I took down a report from a group of nurses after yet another incident, Audrey had an idea.

"How about you dress like a woman, Joe? Then perhaps he would flash you."

I was appalled. I'm taller than average, heavily muscled, and I have undeniably hairy legs. I couldn't fool anyone.

"That's a great idea," said Ginny, and the other girls nodded, looking hopeful. I knew I had to try everything. I checked my watch.

"Okay, this shift leaves in 20 minutes. I'll leave when you do." I pulled off my jacket. "Whadya got for clothes?"

Someone donated an elastic-waist skirt and I borrowed the largest woman's overcoat on the rack. The nurses found some tubular gauze, which I slipped over each leg and taped to my thighs. It was most uncomfortable, and I'm sure it looked quite silly, particularly since my feet were too big for anything but my own shoes. I hoped the darkness would hide most of the oddities. I slung a purse over my arm and tied a kerchief around my huge skull, and walked, surrounded by nurses, into the parking lot.

The next thing you know, here comes my friend. He whistled once, and when I turned toward him, he opened his coat. The fury and frustrations of all those weeks of cat-and-mouse unleashed in me. I grabbed him and threw handcuffs on him so fast, I don't think he had time to blink, and then I hustled him off to the station for booking. I had to chuckle later when I heard him ranting in admiration about the strength of the lady who'd nabbed him.

After that night, I walked Audrey to her car whenever I could. She talked, acted, and dressed with a quiet dignity that continued to draw me to her, but I wouldn't be fooled. Like a trained cop, I stayed on the alert, knowing that at some point the real Audrey would show herself.

We fell into a nightly routine of sharing a snack during Audrey's break. I enjoyed chatting with her. Occasionally we'd attend hospital-sponsored cook outs or other events together, and that led to a few dates. One evening as I waited in her apartment while she changed for our date, I noticed an open Bible on the table and picked it up.

"What's this for?" I held it out when she returned from the bedroom. "Don't tell me you actually read it."

"Sure," she said. "Every morning."

I was blown away. I'd never known anyone who read the Bible. I'd always considered it off limits. I remember my Catechism teacher telling us that the priests interpreted it for us because we couldn't *possibly* understand it.

Is Audrey for real, or is she trying to show off?

Then Audrey brought me home to meet her mom and dad. They were exactly like her: kind, peaceful, and seemingly transparent. Audrey had her father's chin and her mother's eyes, but it was their mannerisms that threw me off.

Her father insisted I call him Glenn and welcomed me with a bear hug, as if I were family. Beth, her mother, laughed sweetly at all my jokes and served a wonderful dinner. They both asked questions and listened with rapt attention to my answers. I felt as if they honestly cared about me.

This has to be a show; it's too perfect...something is wrong here.

The pieces started to fall in place a few weeks later when Audrey invited me to attend church service with her family, and to an adult Bible study school afterward. I went only because she asked. I'd not stepped foot in a church in years, and I knew I didn't belong there. Church was for weak and naïve people who couldn't take care of themselves.

Despite recognizing that same look of peace and gentleness on the faces in the congregation that I'd seen in Audrey's family, I smirked at these people from behind my hymnal, and at Audrey too, for that matter. They'd never make it in my world. In my world, might and cleverness trumped faith and kindness at every turn, and the meek were mowed down by the powerful.

I believed that the only reason people like Audrey were free to go to church and sing like this was because I and my fellow police officers were out there in the real world, keeping the city safe.

Although I didn't know it at the time, that so-called real world was about to test my mettle, so much so that I've referred to the event ever since as, "my dance with Death."

It began when Capt. Carson briefed us on a recent robbery, describing the victim as a "gentleman citizen" who had been accosted at Shakey's bar. The captain's slight smirk told us the man had started out looking for trouble and wound up a victim.

According to the report, a bartender named Ralph had a reputation for finding women to help out-of-towners "meet their needs." So our man went to Shakey's, and found Ralph, who agreed to arrange a meeting. Instead of bringing his victim to a woman, Ralph brought him to an apartment nearby and took all his money at gunpoint.

When the captain finished briefing, he looked directly at me; this was right up my alley, and he knew it.

"Anybody want to take this case?"

Danger, deceit, intrigue—what's not to love? My hand shot up.

I dressed in loose trousers, an "average Joe" sport coat, shirt, and tie. I couldn't let Ralph suspect I was a cop, so I left my shoulder holster behind, wedging my .38 special into a leg holster instead. Then I grabbed some marked money, or bills with recorded serial numbers, and I headed to Shakey's.

I didn't want to appear anxious so I smoked and made small talk for a while, letting Ralph check me out. When I let slip that I was here on business and that Buffalo's sure a lonely town, Ralph took the bait.

"I've got just the thing." He leaned toward me over the counter. "I know a girl who can make you feel right at home...I can take you to her for $100."

"Whoa!" I glanced at a few nearby tables, going for the nervous-but-savvy look. Then I lowered my voice. "You're not dealing with a new guy here. I want to see the girl first, and when I know she's for real, I'll give you the money."

"No problem," he said. The next thing I knew, we were heading to his apartment, which was only a few blocks away. Instead of bringing me inside, he stopped in the yard and snatched up a football that was lying on the ground and tossed it at me.

"Go long!" He grinned.

It was a test. He knew I'd have to take off my jacket, and then he could check whether I had a gun. I stripped off the jacket and tried to act natural. I've never leapt with so much caution. All my focus was on keeping my pant leg from rising to reveal the pistol. It must have looked extremely odd, but after a few tosses I guess he was satisfied that I was just an awkward receiver, and we headed inside.

Ralph introduced me to a scantily clad young woman who had to be in her 20s. I don't remember her name, but I can clearly recall her two small children, the oldest around 3. She ushered them into a back room. I followed her into the room and patted the kids on the head, trying to take in every detail. The walls were thin, and the windows were at floor level and wide open; only a flimsy expandable screen kept those kids from falling out. They must have been routinely exposed to this sort of activity, so I tried not to think about their situation.

I returned to Ralph in the other room.

"So, you got the money?"

Pulling out two $50 bills, I nodded, and asked the girl if she was ready. In answer, she started disrobing, right there in front of Ralph. When she was nearly nude, I showed her my badge and said, "You're under arrest. I'm a police officer."

My words were still in the air when Ralph charged at me from across the room, reaching into his pocket. I bent down and pulled my gun from the holster, coming up with it as he came down with a knife. We grabbed each other's wrists, but he was definitely the stronger one. His hand crushed my finger against the trigger. He turned my gun toward me.

"Good Lord, I'm going to be killed by my own gun!"

I remembered the children in the next room, separated by only a partition.

A stray bullet could kill one of them, too.

I fought to maintain my wits. Ralph may have been stronger, but I was taller and had better leverage. It took nearly all my weight to hold down his knife hand, and everything I had left to move the gun before it went off. The shot rang so loudly in my ears that for a while I could hear nothing else. I was still bent over, but Ralph wasn't on me anymore.

Am I injured? I straightened cautiously and looked around.

Ralph lay on the floor, dead.

My partners crashed into the room as soon as the gun went off. They ushered me away and secured the scene. I had to appear before a grand jury because it was a homicide. The jury deemed my actions justifiable. We learned during the investigation that Ralph had escaped from an asylum for the criminally insane.

Did it change me?

I took a life. He would have killed me. Still, as much as I believed he brought this on himself, I felt remorse over his wasted life. It bothered me to know I was responsible for his death. And for what? Prostitution charges were minimal. Chances are he would have received probation, or at the most, six months to a year in a county jail.

But did it change me?

I don't think so. I've since reconciled with the idea that one of us was destined to die that day, and I was the lucky one. At the time, though, this event only served to bolster my opinion of myself. Was I hot stuff or what? I'd fought a battle that could have gone either way and I came out on top.

When I left Ralph's apartment, I drove straight to the hospital to tell Audrey what had happened. She already knew. She always knew. Ambulance drivers were *such* blabbermouths. Still, I appreciated the concern on her face and the extra kisses I garnered for my ordeal.

Ralph's death made headlines in the local papers, but the event was quickly overshadowed by a larger, more daring crime, one that affected the entire city.

On December 29, 1964, two unmasked men strolled into the Buffalo City Hall treasury office in the middle of the afternoon, slugged the city treasurer over the head with the butt end of a pistol, and took off with nearly $300,000 to a stolen car waiting outside. This was a lot of money back then, and the thieves' timing was strategically significant. The heist occurred at the end of the month, at a time when most people paid their bills with cash and checks. The thieves knew the treasury would likely have a lot of money on hand that day.

It had been an organized crime heist, that much was clear. It fit the Syndicate's method of operation: case a job, assess the security system, devise a plan, and then find some poor schmuck to carry it out. They had a great pool of poor schmucks to choose from, most of whom were gamblers so far in debt to the Mafia they'd never get out. All it took was a few words: "Hey, you wanna' square up?"

What gambler wouldn't leap at a chance to erase his slate? To make the offer more enticing, everyone in "the business" understood that those who refused such a deal would somehow meet up with goons who would work them over. Most people would take the gamble rather than risk two broken legs and two broken arms. Besides, if you get away with it, not only does it square your debt, but you could walk away with some extra cash. Better to take the chance and commit the crime.

The City Hall Holdup marred Buffalo's record so badly that its top officials (the mayor and the police commissioner in particular) made catching the criminals priority. Our police department had a capable robbery squad, but despite a thorough investigation, they came up with nothing. By February, they hit a wall. The police commissioner pulled everyone from the ranks and put them on the case—every plain-clothes officer, the narcotics folks, all of us in Vice, and anyone else who might be able to help.

As it turned out, I had the breakthrough secret weapon they needed: a small-time gambler named Pete Giovanni.

Informants don't fall out of the sky, mind you. A good police officer grooms informants by granting favors over time. If someone is busted for drunk driving or smoking a joint, you speak up for him in court. He appreciates it. Instead of hard time, he gets probation. By interceding, you gain a favor down the road.

I met Giovanni when he got mixed up in a prostitution bust. Wrong place, wrong time sort of thing. I let him go with a warning.

A few weeks later, I was in court testifying on another case when I saw him there. I stopped to chat and learned he'd been busted for peanuts. I reacted as if it were major deal, and said I'd go talk to the judge and see if I could do anything.

"If I do this, though," I said, "you owe me big time."

"Anything, anything," he said. He'd thought he was going to jail forever.

The judge gave him probation and sent him away.

So, there I was, about a year later, working down my list of informants, and I called on Giovanni. As luck would have it, he knew about the City Hall contract. One of his prostitute friends was dating someone who had been approached to help with the job but had chickened out because it was too big. She told Giovanni the name of a man who accepted the job. He gave us that name, Pascal Calabrese, and said the rest is up to us.

It wasn't a solid lead, being fourth-hand information, but it was more than we'd had in a long time so we started pounding pavement. Turns out there were two people named Pascal Calabrese. One was a law-abiding citizen without even a parking ticket to his name; the other was his cousin, who went by the nickname "Paddy," and who had a less-than-spotless record. We got mug shots of both people, mixed them with others, and showed them to the City Hall clerks. They picked out Paddy easily. It was February 19, nearly two months after the hold-up, and he was out of town—in California planning another mob heist that we would learn about later. We put out a warrant for Paddy's arrest, and when he returned we locked him up.

Paddy's attorney knew how to play the game. He used the media like a pro, claiming Paddy was being railroaded, that he hadn't even been in Buffalo that day, and that the police had planted the mug shot. The papers were eating it all up. Even my boss started to worry.

"You're sure you've got the right guy?"

"Not the slightest doubt, Captain."

In the weeks leading up to Paddy's trial, I received a strange phone call from someone who said he'd been a high school friend of mine. He referred to a school social we'd attended together, using overly specific descriptions, which only made me suspicious. Out of the blue, he brought up Paddy's upcoming arraignment.

"Joe," he said, "I'm calling for some pals of mine. If you can, before you go to trial, just create a doubt. Say you're not sure it was Paddy. We'll send any amount of money, within reason, to any bank in the world."

Of course, I said I couldn't do it. He tried a different tactic.

"Because I'm your friend," he said. "I want to tell you that something could happen to your children, perhaps both of them, and perhaps your ex-wife."

"Well," I said, "Now *you* have a problem, because if anything does happen to my family, legitimate accident or not, I will go to the police arsenal and check out a machinegun. I know where you and your pals hang out, and until they get me, we're going to have some fun."

I tell you this, not to prove I was a tough guy or anything—I was nothing—but because it shows my nature back then. This man threatened my life and my family; I didn't play games.

The man hung up, and I never heard from him again, but just the same, I took all precautions to protect my ex-wife and the kids. My brother Sam, the hot-tempered perfectionist, stayed with my family during the trial. He brought along his shotgun and Baron, the family German Sheppard. He also brought his wife, Ceal, who had a pistol and knew how to use it. Outside the home, I knew a team of trusted men watched the house.

The court convicted Paddy Calabrese. He waited in jail a long time before his sentence came through. The Syndicate dropped him like a hot potato, which turned out to be a bad idea a few years down the road, because the police used that wait time to befriend Paddy. More on that later.

For my role in apprehending Calabrese, the department promoted me to detective sergeant, and city officials awarded me the Distinguished Service Medal at the next annual Policeman's Ball. Unfortunately, by the date of the ball I was deeply entrenched in an undercover assignment, complete with full beard and shoulder-length hair. There was no way I could walk up the dais without blowing my cover.

The commissioner suggested my son, Joey, accept the award in my place. Joey was 10 at the time, and quite the little man. Once I agreed, I couldn't NOT witness this moment, so on the night of the ball I dressed as a building worker and made my way to an unpopulated area of the building to watch the banquet from the wings.

When the commissioner announced, "Receiving the award for his Dad is Joseph Tuttolomondo Jr.," a lump formed in my chest as I watched Joey step up and cross the dais before hundreds of people. He stood tall while the mayor pinned the medal on him amid deafening applause. I tried to blink away my tears, but, truth be told, a father's pride needs no apology.

By 1965, I was at the top of my game, arresting 2-3 prostitutes a day. I took great pains to separate myself from their personal stories. I could never fully understand what would make a young woman give herself over to prostitution. I tried hard not to care.

Then I met Didi, a beautiful young woman, about 18 or 19 years old, with blue eyes that sparkled with life, golden hair that fell to her waist, and a lovely figure. When I arrested her for prostitution, I could tell she was new to the trade.

Perhaps this one can be saved.

I accompanied her to the courtroom and stood beside her. As she listened to the charges, the seriousness of her situation sank in, and her tears of remorse broke my heart. I couldn't help but care what happened to her.

"Your honor, I'm so sorry." Didi looked like a child in front of the judge's bench. "I've never done this before; I really needed the money, and I thought—" She wiped her eyes with a tissue. "I'll never do it again!"

I believed her story. So did the judge. He put her on probation, and gave her a strong lecture about making good choices. Through grateful tears, she promised that she would get a job and stay on the right path. I felt good about Didi's chances.

About 6 months later, while working a telephone-prostitution sting, I called a number we'd received through a tip line, and told the woman who answered that I was a salesman in town on business.

"Someone gave me your number," I said. "If I've got the wrong person, I'm terribly sorry and I'll hang up, but on the off chance that he gave me a good tip, I'd really like to avail myself. I come into town every week and it would be nice to have a friend like you."

"Yes Sir, this is the right number." She had a lovely voice.

We arranged to meet at a downtown hotel, and I arrived early so I could watch her from the corner of the lobby. When she walked in, I took one look at her and felt as if I'd been sucker punched. It was Didi—not the Didi I remembered, but a sickly, repulsive, drug-addict of a girl. Her sunken eyes looked empty, her hair was a mess, and her emaciated arms were scarred with track marks. She didn't recognize me at all.

I couldn't believe that sweet child had deteriorated to this point in so short a time. I became angry, remembering how beautiful and full of potential she'd been. I was angry at being fooled by her tears, angry at the world for putting her in this position, and angry at how quickly she'd been sucked into addiction.

What became of Didi? I'll never know. Some social workers got her into rehab, but I didn't keep tabs. I guess I didn't want to be disappointed again. Instead, I took all my anger and directed it at the drug trade.

Narcotics 101

1965-1970

To the nation, Didi's story represented merely an insignificant footnote in the rapidly unfolding story of America's drug addiction. For me, however, it marked a huge change in my life's trajectory. Watching this sweet, innocent-looking young woman transform into an emaciated wretch almost overnight really got to me. I knew I couldn't save her, or for that matter, any of the other addicts I met in the course of my duties. Their problems were too big for me. I wasn't a counselor, or a doctor, or a social worker.

On the other hand, I was a darned good cop, so if I was going to make any difference, I would have to start there. I wondered if Didi's story could have been changed if she'd been removed from her environment, or if we could have somehow gotten ahead of the drug suppliers. Six months after clamping my handcuffs around Didi's tiny wrists for the second time, I interviewed with the chief of narcotics for a transfer to his squad. It was late 1965, just as President L.B. Johnson's administration was connecting the dots between America's rising crime rates and its increasing drug abuse. His staff created a task force to search for national answers to local problems.

I had a solid reputation by then as an earnest and trustworthy police officer, with 200-plus arrests in Vice, not to mention cracking the City Hall Holdup case, so my transfer request was quickly approved. Before I could hit the streets, however, I had a lot to learn about the business.

The drug scene in Buffalo, as in many of America's cities, was changing daily. Although marijuana use continued to climb steadily, a host of new drugs were gaining popularity. Timothy Leary, Ken Kesey, and other prominent proponents of mind-altering drug use were on the national stage proclaiming that LSD and PCP could help us expand our minds to their "natural potential." Their praises, combined with medical journal warnings to stay away from these drugs (the same magazines that a year or so earlier had been extolling their potential in the field of psychiatry), piqued the interest of America's middle class and ushered in an era of recreational drug use. An alarming number of students, athletes, housewives, and truck drivers were turning to amphetamines because they heard it would increase their endurance and performance, and help combat depression. In reality, the perceived benefit they attained from these "pep-pills" was just overstimulation of the nervous-system; users would typically either overestimate their own capabilities (sometimes with dire consequences) or they would stay awake beyond the point of exhaustion, becoming lost in a surreal wasteland of hallucinations and paranoia.

LSD was easy to synthesize, and therefore quite abundant. However, it was heroin (Didi's drug) that caused those of us in law enforcement the greatest concern. The addictive and destructive qualities of heroin were frightening.

Heroin use in America, which had noticeably subsided during World War II, resurged to alarming levels in the late 60s and early 70s. Much of the credit for this revival goes to Corsican/French connections in Organized Crime that started transporting opium through Turkey and into the United States across Canada's southern border. Additionally, Asian smuggling networks established by U.S. servicemen during the Vietnam War were bringing sizeable amounts of opium into the country. Often, the heroin was smuggled in the bodies of fallen soldiers returning to the States. Customs never inspected this precious cargo.

In Buffalo, and across the country, the stage had been set for the national War on Drugs. The Bureau of Narcotics and Dangerous Drugs (a predecessor to today's Drug Enforcement Agency) was given federal-level responsibility for resolving the nation's drug problem. Local police departments like mine provided critical leg work.

If we were to succeed at all, we had to get to the sources: those who supplied the street dealers, and those who supplied *them*, and so on, up the ladder. The street dealers' ranks were increasing, and they were well sheltered from the law (as well as through the *omertà*-like code). It was nearly impossible to get anyone to testify against a dealer. Even someone who was "burned" with phony or poor-quality drugs would rather go to another dealer than turn snitch. People who testified against a dealer tended to end up with serious bodily injury, death, or (even worse) no one to buy drugs from. Word spread quickly in the drug community.

The Bureau provided police agencies across the country with extensive counterdrug training, teaching us how to identify various narcotics, paraphernalia, ingestion methods, and their effects on users. We also learned to navigate the developing accumulation of Federal laws and regulations that both helped and hindered our efforts. Finally, we had to learn how to assimilate into the street scene, familiarizing ourselves with the current lingo and mannerisms and developing courses of action we could take that would be acceptable among pushers and dealers.

I was assigned to a three-man team. We were ready, or so we hoped. We grew our hair to shoulder-length and dressed like the youth of our culture, calling ourselves the Mod Squad, after a popular television show of the era. I wore an old Air Force field jacket with the hood down to hide my name on the back. My partners both wore beat up leather jackets. Anyone would think we were three thugs looking for trouble.

My regular partners were Mickey Serano and Al Dembrowski. Like me, they volunteered for the assignment. Mick a short, wiry, intensely focused man with a drug addict brother, seemed driven to put dealers behind bars. I could always tell when he'd heard from his brother or seen him on the streets. He'd come to work, eyes gleaming with defiance, just daring the world to mess with him. I guess he thought if he worked just a little harder to arrest those scumbags, perhaps he could stop his brother's supply. I thought the same way sometimes, when I met people like Didi.

If we could just stem the supply...

We didn't fully realize back then that the supply was, and still is, endless.

Dembrowski was our intimidator—nicest guy you'd ever want to meet, but you wouldn't know it to look at him. His weathered face sported so much character it made you wonder what the other guy looked like. He towered over Mick and me at about six-feet-six. His mere presence was usually enough to settle a situation. On more than a few occasions we convinced a rather tough pusher it would be better for him to spill the beans than for us to leave him alone in the room with Dembrowski.

I was the meticulous one. A detail man. I recorded everything we did as if my life depended on it. I made sure, once we nabbed someone, that our case was air-tight. I insisted we follow the book, which meant closing every loophole, particularly when requesting a search warrant. The paperwork took me longer than some people to complete because it hurt my eyes, but I turned in thorough reports.

Search warrants were essential tools for any narcotics officer. Only a few years before I joined the team, Ohio police acting without a warrant had stormed the home of a woman named Dollree Mapps, looking for a suspected bomber; instead they found incriminating documents unrelated to their search, for which they arrested Mapps. The ensuing court battle became a landmark case; its findings were adopted by New York law, establishing that any evidence collected without a warrant is inadmissible in court. While I agreed in principle that this measure was vital in protecting citizens' rights, it created a new level of bureaucracy for police officers.

So, of course, we became well-versed in search warrant procedures. If our investigation led to a home at which drugs might be present, we'd submit what we considered "reasonable and probable grounds" for a search. If he agreed with our assessment, the judge would give us a warrant to execute—sometimes on a dwelling or vehicle, and other times on an individual. For routine busts, this was typically sufficient. However, if we thought we might have to kick down the doors and surprise the residents to keep them from flushing drugs down the toilet, or worse, grabbing weapons and barricading themselves for a shoot-out, well, that required a "no-knock" warrant. In these cases we had to provide concrete evidence to convince the judge that drugs or weapons were present or that lives were in danger.

We acquired concrete evidence by making undercover drug purchases. We could also ask a reliable informant, someone we'd worked with previously, to make a purchase. Working with an informant was tricky, because we had to be absolutely certain he wasn't using us to settle a score. Before sending him in, we'd give his body more than a basic pat-down, lest he smuggle drugs *onto* the scene and fake a buy to frame our suspect.

In a typical house bust, every officer takes a room the second we burst through the door, because residents throughout the house start throwing objects out the windows, flushing material down the toilets, and shoving stuff under the beds. It's all evidence. We had to be careful about chain of custody. If we found something that might be incriminating, we didn't touch it. Instead, we'd call for the evidence man who would pick it up, bag it and record all the info about it. The chain of possession was paramount because a defense attorney could, and would, demand to question everyone who handled a particular item to determine whether it had been compromised in any way. By using an evidence man, I could testify about anything we found and honestly say we hadn't touched it.

In some cases, new regulations worked in our favor. For instance, in the early years, time was our biggest enemy. There was nothing more frustrating than working for weeks to line up a suspect and stage a "buy," either in our undercover personalities or through a reliable informant (which allowed us to stay incognito), only to be told after presenting our findings to a judge that we had to wait. Sometimes for a week or more. With every passing day our chances of nabbing a dealer worsened. One brief out-of-state incident changed all that. Apparently, a week after staging a buy at an apartment, some police officers (I believe they were from Colorado) were granted permission to conduct a no-knock through the wall of an apartment, not knowing that the dealer had moved away, or that the guy inside was a former Marine who had just moved in. As soon as they crashed through, that Marine grabbed his .45 and shifted to high alert. Amid the shouting and confusion that followed, either side could have pulled a trigger. Instead, the officers managed to identify themselves and get the Marine to put his gun down. Cooler heads prevailed that time, but it turned into another court case, this time mandating that warrants be executed within 24 hours of obtaining the evidence. We liked that change.

The three of us blended into Buffalo's city culture by joining picket lines, hanging out at park gatherings, bumming cigarettes—anything to be part of the streets. It was a dangerous lifestyle. My biggest fear was that I'd be discovered. They called undercover officers narcs, and didn't exactly speak kindly of them. Not only that, but once your face is recognized, word spreads like wildfire and you're of little undercover use.

Dembrowski wasn't with us the night I got whacked over the head. He had some business at home. Chances are, we wouldn't have been attacked if our enforcer had been there.

Mick and I were in a bar that Friday night. He played some pool while I sat across the room on a stool in a phone booth. The typical din of loud drunks and a bellowing juke box made conversation practically impossible, but I wanted to check in with Audrey. With one eye I watched the mirror behind the bar, keeping Mick in sight despite the cloud of cigarette smoke that hung in the air. My coin clanged into the slot just as a commotion erupted at the pool table. I saw the men around Mick working up an argument and one guy took a swing. Mick went down and both guys started beating on him. I raced over to help, but a third man came from nowhere and cracked a pool cue over my head.

I felt my world going dark and I could no longer hear the noise of the bar, but I fought the darkness with everything I had. Even as I began to crumple, my thoughts were about keeping my cover. I hit the floor knowing that I couldn't stay down, or else I was a dead man. Slowly, at first, then with a rush, the noise returned but I still couldn't see. Blood from the wound on my head seeped into my eyes. I had something, or was it someone, locked in my right arm, which I held secure with my left hand. It was someone! Later an onlooker told me that when the thug struck me with the cue, I turned around and grabbed him and we both went down.

I was trying to clear the blood from my eyes when he broke loose and ran for the door. Instinctively I raced after him, regaining my senses and becoming more and more furious at this person with each step. Determined not to let him escape, I caught up to him after running about a city block and lunged through the air to tackle him. We rolled around, off the curb, into the street, and onto a manhole cover. It took all I had to stay conscious.

If I lose this fight, he'll put his boots to my head and finish the job he started.

To this day, I have no idea what happened in those minutes, or where the adrenaline came from to get me outside that bar, but the important thing was I caught him. The police arrived and hauled him away, and I raced to Buffalo General to get stitched up. As usual, Audrey knew I was on the way and met me in the emergency room. I had a serious head wound that took eight stitches to close.

The media was hunting for "that guy from the bar." They always found out about these things somehow. I couldn't be seen on camera, and I couldn't miss my usual late-Friday night rendezvous with Mick at the club on Prospect Avenue, or else some of the drug crowd we'd been infiltrating there would put two and two together. Audrey combed my long hair over the bandaged wound and pasted it in place with hairspray, and then I sped home to change my bloody shirt.

I found Mick at the club, nursing a black eye, but none the worse for wear. Apparently, the fight had stopped when I ran out the door. We heard rejoicing in the street and some club buddies who entered after us said some narc had "been taken care of and was almost dead."

Whew!

In retrospect, I can tell you that life among the dopers may be low, but the life of a narc is even lower. It didn't matter to me. I could act noble and repeat the coined phrase, "Somebody has to do it," but the truth is I found the job extremely interesting and quite exciting. Something about walking on the edge of danger satisfied me. It's difficult to verbalize why; perhaps it was the challenge of pitting my street savvy and desire to fight for right against those who lived by their wits pursuing wrong. The high stakes only added to the thrill.

While we were undercover, Mick, Dembrowski, and I reported to our supervisor several times throughout the day and night. We discussed our activities and informed him of any recent progress, and let him know if we needed supplies or support, like money for buys, another apartment, staged harassment from the police to impress dealers, etc.

We had apartments and hideouts throughout the city. We had a particularly fruitful place downtown around Allen Street, where drugs were prevalent. Our street friends became accustomed to seeing us there and visited us often. We plastered the walls with rebellious posters, and scattered drug paraphernalia around the place. We wanted them to trust us in case anyone came around asking questions.

We also had access to a nearby drug analysis lab with a covert back entrance in an alleyway. You wouldn't think it was a lab. Still, we were careful never to be seen entering the alley straight from a buy—zig zag, backtrack, stop, turn left, right. These days, police use video cameras to record evidence, and they can test on the spot, but in the 60s, the process was a little more involved. The moment you made a buy, you sent it to the lab, where they determined whether it was heroin or not. If it was, I logged it in and locked it in a safe, for which only I had the combination; if we couldn't get there, I took it to a roaming evidence van, which was our street safe. Taking these precautions enabled us to show the judge a distinct chain of custody, with every step tagged and logged.

In 1968, a reporter from the Buffalo Evening News patrolled with us for a few weeks. At first he was a bit too clean for our taste, but he dirtied up a bit and went a few days without shaving to get ready. We told him he could stay as long as he didn't blow our cover. He received one heck of an education while he was with us. One night we were all outside a nightclub when a pretty young girl approached and asked if she could join us. We treated her badly, taunting and jeering, calling her a child until she stormed away. I could tell the reporter was shaken.

"For Pete's sake, she couldn't have been more than 17!" He stared after her in disbelief. "And yet she's so willing to throw her life away!"

There was another young girl who shook him up. She claimed to be 20 but turned out to be a 15-year-old runaway from Massachusetts. The girl was strung out and sick from the drugs she'd been taking; we found her roaming around downtown, a waif-thin child with matted hair and sunken eyes. We sat her down and fed her a good meal while the police back at the station ran a trace and figured out who she was. Then we called her parents and paid the fare to send her back home.

The reporter accompanied us to numerous drug buys on the University of Buffalo campus and to crowded parties where he watched young men and women pass around marijuana joints and LSD, swaying to mood music while light shows danced on the walls and ceilings to heighten the trip experience. Some of the kids were so stoned they just sat and stared; others were clearly hallucinating—talking to lamps, crying, swatting the air. It hurt to watch girls leave with boys they'd only just met. I figured the reporter must have been a father because that sort of scene always rattled him. We'd stay long enough to identify some 20-year-old college lad or local businessman who was supplying the drugs and then arrange for the police to raid the place.

The reporter was so moved by the activity he witnessed that, after our investigation ended, he wrote a full page feature article about us, trying to wake parents up to the dangers their children were facing in this city. LSD proponents accused us of harassing partiers, claiming the drugs were harmless. Well, they never had to stop a young man from sticking his hands into an industrial-sized oscillating fan because he thought it was a clock and he needed to adjust the time.

Despite making many small-time busts at parties and night clubs, drugs kept flooding into the city. We knew there were some major criminals operating right under our noses, and we wanted to take them down. We specifically wanted to crack the code regarding a particular high-traffic area on Buffalo's East Side—a close-knit community that would not buy from or sell to strangers. We'd been on the streets for some time without a single nibble from this area. The only way in was to become one of them, but that was easier said than done.

In 1968, Dembrowski and I got this idea to stage a fake nab, trusting the criminal brotherhood to protect two of "their own" in a time of need. We figured if we could make it look as if we were being arrested in view of some prominent criminals, we might find a way in.

It sounded good on paper. Of course, that's why they invented the phrase, "best laid plans…"

We worked it out to what we thought was the smallest detail: Dembrowski and I would walk down the street and some officers driving by in a squad car would jump out and nab us, shake us down, and "find" something. Then, before they could get us into the car, we'd break away and run past the warehouses.

At first, all went well. A patrolman friend of mine named Ben was in the squad car, and he made sure to sound the siren to attract attention. Dembrowski and I faked a dart away but allowed them to nab us. Ben grabbed me and quickly patted me down, pulling a bag from my pocket. He held the bag up to the other officer, who was searching Dembrowski.

"Look what I found." Ben's remark signaled me to run. I slammed Ben with my elbow, pushed his partner aside and took off …right toward a rookie patrolman walking his beat.

Apparently, nobody had thought to include the patrolman in our plans. As soon as he saw what was going on, he pulled out his nightstick and blocked my way. I ducked under the stick but he was well trained; he grabbed me, threw me to the ground, patted me down, and came up with my gun.

Back at the squad car, quick thinking on Ben's part saved the day. He let Dembrowski "fight" his way free and race over to us, then re-tackled him in front of the patrolman, hissing at the poor rookie, "They're narcotics agents! Play possum and let 'em go!"

That patrolman should have won an award for the way he hammed it up, groaning and writhing in pain after I faked a kick to his gut and took off. I ran past an old warehouse and heard an urgent voice say, "Quick, in here!"

All I could see was a hand gesturing wildly from a doorway. I raced into the warehouse and was ushered down to the cellar through a maze of doors and hallways. I didn't have my gun if anything happened. I didn't have cover. Nobody knew where I was. I was certain not even Dembrowski saw me enter the building. I said a quick prayer in my desperation, although I hardly believed I was doing anything other than talking to myself.

The warehouse turned out to be a major hub of East Side underground activity. I recognized faces I'd only seen in mug shots, and heard names of people we'd thought were "untouchables" being tossed around as easily as one would discuss family. I stayed the night, chatting with my new buddies while we waited for the coast to clear, and by morning I had gained acceptance into the area. Eventually, they made me one of them. I brought my own guys in, and we started making buys.

Gaining acceptance into the drug culture is a major coup for a team of narcotics agents. There were, however, two dominant problems. First, we couldn't take drugs, yet we had to convince them we were users. We did a lot of pretending, smoking artificial marijuana made of ground basil leaves and palming speed and other pills to make everyone think we were okay with the light stuff. We then had to act like the guys around us who really *had* taken them. We performed nightly, like actors in a bad play.

We drew the line at the heavy stuff; shooting up was never an option. Instead, we made it known that because we were dealers we couldn't get hung up on anything. This was an accepted good-business practice; many dealers we worked with abided by the same code.

The second issue was that we couldn't arrest a dealer immediately after we made a buy. Once our identity was divulged, the well would dry up. At the same time, once we built a case on a particular dealer, we couldn't continue buying from him, because we would be supporting his business. So, after collecting enough data for a conviction on a particular dealer, we would either complain that his "stuff" was of poor quality and go on to another dealer or we'd "order up" an amount the dealer couldn't supply. Usually the dealer would then take us to his own source, and the stakes would go higher.

Chiefy was a big dealer. Not just physically (although I have to say he was the biggest, most ornery man I ever met), but also because he moved a lot of heroin. Lest anyone be inclined to think Chiefy was an Indian, he was not. In fact, in all my years on the job I never saw or heard of Indians using or selling drugs. No, this man was Chiefy because he did big-time business. He dealt in bundles, whereas up until that time we'd dealt primarily in packets (a bundle was 25 packets; a double bundle was 50 packets).

Early in our stint on the East Side, I bought a bundle from Chiefy that almost cost me my life.

As soon as Chiefy and I made the exchange, I grabbed Mick and we high-tailed it out of there with the stash, zig-zagging our way to the police lab to verify it was heroin and determine its quality and origin. (We could tell which country, and sometimes even which *region* it came from, by the strain of poppy seed.) This particular bundle was a burn, which meant the lab found no presence of heroin in any of the packets. They were trying us.

We immediately returned to the area and I confronted Chiefy.

"Man, this stuff is a burn," I said. "I laid it on someone and it was cold."

"Tough sh--," he replied.

"Make it right or give me my bread back" I said. A crowd had gathered to watch the action. Many were dealers. If I backed down, my chance of ever getting the real stuff again was zero.

Chiefy pulled a switchblade knife and said: "F- off sucker."

As his knife went to my chest, I pulled out my own switch blade and put it to his.

"If you do me, I'll do you and nobody wins," I said. "Just make the deal right, give me the good stuff or give my money back."

I don't know why—maybe I looked serious; I certainly hoped I looked serious—but he backed off, put his knife away, and gave me another bundle. This time the lab analysis tested positive for heroin.

We stayed undercover there for six months, making buys and recording names and networks. Most of the dealers answered to nick names, but we stuck with the task and just kept learning as much as we could. When the time came to make some arrests, we indicted 101 dealers. We had warrants for many others, most of whom had fled the area. Some were never caught.

Chiefy was one of the 101. I remember arresting him. He stands out in my memory because he had put the knife to me. Later, when I saw Chiefy in prison, I recognized him right away.

Netting the 101 was a major coup for the city's law enforcement, but it paled in comparison to what was happening in organized crime. As the 1960s came to a close, Buffalo's crime syndicate started to shut down as well.

Much of the *Black Hand's* downfall can be attributed to the leadership's ill-fated decision to break one of their own rules after the December 1964 City Hall robbery. It had taken two months for us to identify, locate, and then arrest "Paddy" Calabrese for the crime. In the time between the robbery and his arrest in February 1965, Paddy had been working with the Syndicate on the details to pull off an armored car jewelry heist involving California's Beverly Hilton Hotel, for an expected payout of $400,000. When word reached the Syndicate that we were looking for Paddy for the City Hall robbery, they called off the hotel heist. Paddy returned from California and turned himself in, confident he'd receive top cover from his crime family. Although he knew all the details of the planned California heist and names of those involved, he abided by the *Omertà* code for nearly two years, keeping his secret throughout the questioning, the trial, and even afterward while awaiting his sentencing. He honestly believed Mafia lawyers would come to his rescue.

They never did.

In September 1966, when Paddy was handed his prison sentence, he finally accepted that his "family" had left him out to dry. In retaliation, he offered to testify against his former employers in exchange for release and protection. Thanks to his testimony, in June 1967, Buffalo's Mafia boss Stefano Magaddino and at least four other prominent members of organized crime families in Buffalo and California were indicted on conspiracy charges related to the aborted jewelry heist and three bank robberies. Their trial received significant national media attention. The government gave Paddy a new identity and whisked him off to start a new life with his girlfriend and three step-children.

This event brought national attention to the Federal Witness Protection plan, and sparked a chain of similar organized crime betrayals that enabled the government to put many more high-level criminals behind bars. A few years later, a dramatic story unfolded as the Canadian father of Paddy's step-children fought unsuccessfully for visitation rights, even bringing a lawsuit against the U.S. government. The international ordeal culminated in the 1976 book, and subsequent movie, "Hide in Plain Sight."

I don't know if my work as a police officer helped soften my father's view of the world, but I know he was proud of me. Well into his 70s, Pa would walk down to Prospect Park nearly every day to meet up with friends and talk about old times. He'd carry clipped articles about me and show them around. He lived to see me appointed Narcotics Bureau Chief in 1968, and clipped that article as well.

Pa never expressed worry for me, even after hearing about the City Hall hold up. After the Organized Crime folks were indicted, Pa and I were sitting together one afternoon when he put his hand on mine. I looked up, surprised to see tears in his eyes.

"You made *Omertà* die. Bravo, my son."

All traces of fear had left his face, leaving only peace and pride.

Pa died in February, 1969, at age 82. I still miss him. I know now that if I could be only half the man my father was, I would be a whole man.

Grabbing the Brass Ring

1970-1975

I began the 1970s on a personal and professional high, with a new job, a new family, and a new life.

My boss was elected Erie County Sheriff and asked me and another agent, John Duffy, to come with him to help train agents for the county Narcotics Squad. A little more than a year later, when he needed someone to lead his 13-man squad, he appointed me as his Narcotics Chief. The police force granted me a one-year leave of absence to take the position, and extended that leave every year while he was sheriff; he continuously won reelection so I received annual extensions.

I was also newly married. Despite my sixth sense and my suspicious nature, I never did find anything wrong with Audrey. She was exactly who she seemed to be: a good woman, raised by a good family. I'd been waiting for that moment when her caring, selfless façade would come crashing down and reveal what she really wanted from me, but it never did. I enjoyed the trusting feeling I experienced around her, which at times bothered me greatly because I'd taught myself not to trust. I'd also sworn to never remarry, but there I was, asking for her hand.

To this day, I can't imagine why a kind, demure woman like Audrey would marry a tough guy like me. She knew what she was getting into, marrying a cop. She had bandaged enough of us up—most of us more than once—and had heard enough stories to have no sugar-coated ideas about my job. (Soon after we were married, she came home one day and found a bathtub full of blood with a soaking shirt in it. I'd been hit in the head and bled onto the shirt; I left it to soak and went back to work without thinking to tell her what had happened.) She also knew that police officers worked long hours, particularly in my line of work, and that I'd be pretty much on call around the clock.

And yet, she said yes.

We married in June of 1969. Audrey's parents gave us an acre of land on their farm in Lockport, a quiet little town 30 miles outside Buffalo, and we built a home there. My son, Joey, came to live with us, giving me an instant family. With Joey and Audrey in my life, I had to wake up and make some personal changes; I didn't want to blow it. We attended Sunday services at Audrey's church, the Christian & Missionary Alliance Church (where I tried to stay awake), and I attended an adult Sunday school after the service, where I usually argued with the teacher. I argued for the sake of argument; I held no strong views about the Bible or its contents. I considered church attendance an obligation and nothing more.

I felt most uncomfortable during the singing. I mouthed the words to every hymn. They meant nothing to me, and they made me feel a bit silly. Redemption. Salvation. Glory and honor. A bunch of foolishness, I thought. In particular, we sang a hymn called "How Great Thou Art." I kept thinking God couldn't be too great, considering all the unhappiness in the world.

As I watched those around me during the service, that familiar sense of superiority resurged. These were nice people, but weak. I still thought they'd be no match against the criminals and creeps I dealt with every day. And yet, they seemed happier than my non-church-going friends.

I was particularly fond of my in-laws, Glenn and Ruth, who were always doing things for others but asked for nothing in return. I knew they were good-hearted people, but I couldn't begin to understand their thinking; didn't they realize that others were just using them? That their generosity only set them up for exploitation?

At the time, I chalked up their happiness to naiveté. Still, sitting with them made attending church easier, although it didn't keep me from nodding off on occasion.

Audrey and her family didn't push me to participate in the church any more than I felt comfortable. This was good, because it probably kept me from turning away. Since then, I've met many people who had religion shoved at them, and they responded by fortifying their defenses. However, I considered CMA their church, not mine.

In addition to setting an example for Joey at church, I wanted him to respect me the way I had respected my father. The only way I thought I'd accomplish that would be to invest time. I attended Joey's school events whenever possible, and I spent as much time alone with him as I could. We even had season tickets to watch the Bills play football.

In the winters, Joey and I enjoyed taking off on a pair of second-hand snow mobiles I'd acquired. Flying across the land left us exhilarated and the shared experience opened doors for conversation over cocoa when we returned. I wanted to ensure he could talk to me about anything, and I do believe we had that relationship in place. I could have done a better job, and I sure wish I'd been around more instead of being so obsessed with my work, but I knew he looked up to me, and he still does today. He even considered going into law enforcement, but that talk stopped after my arrest.

Those were good years. Whenever I could manage to get some time off, Joey and I spent hours in the garage working on projects. Our greatest project, a 1931 Alpha Romero kit car, took more than a year to build because time off was so rare. The kit contained a hood, fenders, and back end. The rest was up to us. It was designed to go on top of a Volkswagen Bug frame, which we found at a junkyard; the body was all beat up, but the frame was in good shape. We built the deck and dashboard—wired it with motorcycle parts for lights—and constructed a carrier for the back. Sam, by then an industrial arts teacher, helped us with the struts, and I was lucky to have a friend who could weld.

An Alpha Romeo dealer sold me a ragtop frame that we cut down to fit the windshield assembly. Another friend who made convertible tops showed me how to make one. I purchased some fabric and pieced that thing together on a sewing machine.

I still have a picture of that car. On the front it looks like it's sporting a big 16-cylinder motor, but that's the trunk and gas tank. It also had super struts coming out of the exhaust pipe—all phony—but boy, was she beautiful.

My projects not only kept me busy, but they gave me a sense that life was more than just police work. Over the years, Joey and I converted a barn on my father-in-law's property into a stable and acquired a few horses. I rode Lady, a fine, 17-hand mare with coal black eyes, and Joey rode Flame, a beautiful red gelding.

We lucked into buying Coco, an old trotter who couldn't qualify for racing and wasn't making his owner any money. I got Coco and two sets of harnesses for about $100. He may not have been a racer, but Coco was great for pulling a cutter over the snow. I refurbished a sleigh from an old piece of junk and hitched him up. He looked fine, and actually pranced through the snow as if he'd found his calling. I renovated an old doctor's carriage for summer outings.

Our entire family, even my in-laws, enjoyed afternoon drives with Coco. For the most part, we'd ride around the property. However, when the weather was nice we would jump on the buggy for a beautiful ride through the Lockport countryside along the Erie Canal and out to the five locks that gave our little town its name. Those locks, built in the 19th century, were mesmerizing and they are still in use today; each raises and lowers canal traffic 12 feet. In its heyday, the lock system enabled large vessels to negotiate a 60-foot change in elevation.

Joey was becoming a man before my eyes. I tried to use what little time we had together to impart values and principles that would help him succeed in life. Of course, a few of my own values and principles needed some adjustment, but I didn't know that. I noticed Joey had the same attitude towards Sunday services as I did, so occasionally I'd sneak away with him on a Sunday morning to go hunting. We especially enjoyed bow hunting (I could take down a pheasant at 50 feet with an arrow). Audrey was none-too-pleased, but we had some great bonding time.

More and more though, I started putting work before family. I'd leave home early, stay late at the office, and when I did have time off, I'd spend it in on projects and hunting. Once, when Audrey asked me to adjust my schedule so we could be together once in a while, I reminded her that she knew what she was getting into when she married me. That didn't go over well. She and Joey stopped holding dinner for me. I'd often come home and find my plate in the fridge. I became accustomed to Audrey's increasingly frequent silent treatments; I never asked her what was wrong. A smarter man would have realized she was crying out from neglect.

Money was still tight, but with my promotion to chief, I was making just over $10,000 a year. Between that and Audrey's nursing salary we were able to meet expenses and still put money aside for Joey's college, now that he was finishing high school.

My only real worries during those days were about my sweet Jenny. For a while it had looked as if she was going to be okay in the world, despite her mental challenges. Her husband, Frank, treated her wonderfully, and they were raising four children. Then Frank lost his job. After Dad died, they moved into the house on Jersey Street and took the second floor over Casper. Still, there was no money coming in; they had to go on Welfare and get food stamps and such. I'd slip Jenny money now and again so she could buy something nice for herself, but she usually put it toward family expenses. The day-to-day stress started taking its toll on her health.

Back on the streets, the 1970s-era drug culture thrived despite, or perhaps because of, a slight weakening within the Organized Crime network. The Witness Protection Program emboldened lower-level criminals to testify against their superiors, creating turmoil and distrust in the ranks. Splits, inside murders, and infighting rose significantly. The organization did not crumble completely, but its power over the city diminished. The ensuing chaos opened the door for independent drug dealers to try their hand in the business.

To combat the increasing drug problem in the 70s, Buffalo and many of the nation's other large cities implemented the "Turn in a Pusher" program, or TiP. The program made it possible for citizens to anonymously report illegal activities in their neighborhoods. Nine times out of ten, when we received a narcotics-related call, I was part of the response.

One February evening, a TiP caller reported a narcotics deal underway in his neighborhood. The caller said the deal was going down in the center of a rural, horseshoe-shaped field off the main highway. Red flags flew up like rocket flares.

An ideal location for an ambush.

We'd already had several calls that night and our folks had been dispatched everywhere, leaving a scant staff at the squad office, an unusual situation that could hardly be called a coincidence. However, when a police officer receives a complaint, he *has* to respond. It's the law, and it's our job. Duffy and I jumped into an unmarked car and headed out.

We turned off the highway onto a dark lane, and wound our way through the neighborhood to the open field. Our senses were on overdrive as we opened the car doors, stepping onto a slushy mess of mud and snow. We could see no tracks on the ground ahead of us, and the night was eerily quiet.

Something was wrong. I knew it in my gut.

Out of the darkness, bullets started flying past us. Across the field, muzzle flashes from two distinct positions lit up the night. Duffy and I dove under the car and hid behind the wheels to return fire, but we couldn't get a good fix on the shooters. After each shot they rolled in unpredictable directions so we couldn't anticipate and shoot ahead of them. We tried—if they rolled right, we'd shoot to the left of the muzzle flash, only to see a flash further to the right. They knew what they were doing.

I had a five-shot, Smith & Wesson .38 "Police Chief's Special" with 10 rounds in reserve, which gave me 15 shots. I went through 14 but saved the last in case they attempted a kamikaze attack. When my bullets ran out, I reached into the car to grab the radio.

"Under fire! Under fire! Officers need help!"

Almost immediately, sirens blared in the distance. Help was speeding toward us from all directions.

Our shooters ceased firing at the first sound of approaching sirens. They must have had a car parked on the road behind them. They sped off and we never found out who it was.

Duffy and I rolled out from under the car and stood up. We got our first look at the damage in the light from arriving police vehicles. The car was *peppered* with bullet holes. By the looks of things, we'd been out-gunned by a wide margin. My only injury was a scratch on my left knee. I should have dropped right then in awed humility and thanked the Lord for delivering me from what could have happened. But I didn't.

Instead I whooped, "Look at my car! Look at those bullet holes!"

I WAS HOT STUFF! I'd survived. I was *the Man*. Duffy and I exchanged high-fives and returned to the Sheriff's department all fired up with adrenaline and bullet-proof bravado. When we briefed the team the next morning, I read awe in the rookies' faces. They all wanted to be me, I could tell.

That ambush was a bit of an anomaly in the overall TiP program. Despite enabling this type of set-up, the program generally helped us. We intercepted many drug deals and other illicit activities through TiP's anonymous callers. On the down side, TiP calls tended to net only small-time criminals and their users. To get to the sources, we still relied on old-fashioned, undercover immersion.

Toward the end of 1971, councilmen, legislators, and businessmen on Buffalo's East Side started complaining to the Buffalo Police and to the Erie County Sheriff's Department about increasing drug trafficking in their area. Our squad joined the police in ramping up for another lengthy undercover infiltration.

Six of us infiltrated the East Side, focusing our attention on a seller named Murch and his girlfriend. We knew he was providing heroin, but could not catch him in a sale, even after 70 buys. He always had a different dealer to send us to. One afternoon, we hung out in his apartment for about four hours, playing cards with his henchmen and pretending to smoke marijuana. We heard his men take eight calls for narcotics deliveries. Although we never caught him making a direct sale, we did learn where he was stashing the drugs and eventually we were able to get him on possession.

By January 1972, after 10 months undercover, we had amassed more than 100 felony warrants, 46 of which were for the sale and possession of heroin. Murch was among the 14 suspects we arrested the first day; we picked up many more on the second.

I was making enemies, but I didn't care. Murch's girlfriend cried, begged, and then cursed me as we clamped handcuffs around her wrists. I felt no pity. She chose this path, just like everyone in those jails chose their paths. Once I got 'em locked up, I didn't give 'em another thought. I figured anyone who ended up in jail deserved to be there, and for some, the keys should be thrown away. There's no room for sympathy in this job.

That emotional stuff just makes you weak.

I never even *wondered* if they were innocent. Sure, I knew that innocent people went to prison, but innocent people were killed in war, too. That's just the way it goes.

If anyone had asked me to name my role models at that time, I would have said, "Role models? Who needs them?" In my world, I *was* the role model. I believed everyone else thought so too, that people wanted to be like me, and that they looked up to me. The devil uses egos like mine, and I was giving him plenty of ammunition to work with.

In 1972, my armor of invincibility failed me when I learned that my brother John had cancer. The news dealt my heart a hard blow. John had been a heavy smoker. He was only 45, a teacher, a husband, a father to an adopted son, and my best friend. The doctors initially thought it was pneumonia, but it progressed. Six weeks after they determined he had advanced-stage lung cancer, John died. It all happened so quickly that it caught me by surprise. I cried hard for the first time since I was a baby. It took a long time to accept. I'm still not over it.

After that, I felt a little more respect for life's fragility. In awe of how swiftly John's disease had spread, I tried to quit smoking, but I couldn't kick the habit. That was an angry season for me. I didn't hold God responsible for John's death, but I did wonder why he didn't do anything about it. It made no sense; this made a mockery of all those sermons I'd been dozing through on Sunday mornings. The good guys were supposed to inherit the earth; the scumbags were supposed to crash and burn. John was so young, and he was a good man. If God is so wonderful, why didn't the Murches of this world die of cancer instead of people like John? Wouldn't that solve everything?

Yet, instead of dying off, the bad guys seemed to be multiplying. We'd no sooner put one behind bars when two others would rise up to take his place. And they were moving off the streets and further into society. Dealers were infiltrating area high schools, tourist resorts, and anywhere else they could find a crowd.

In June of 1972, Duffy and I brokered a huge deal in Buffalo's Southtowns area, shutting down a major supplier for local youths. We confiscated $67,000 worth of heroin and 33 pounds of marijuana that the dealers had been growing in a three-quarter acre plot near their house. They had even built drying ovens—five-foot square steel boxes with smokestacks attached—so they could prepare the marijuana for sale on-site. As we continued to buy in the region, we arrested younger and younger users. In one week, we netted five young men 16-18 years old; most were students at a nearby high school.

We stayed busy that summer. The local papers ran stories on many of our raids, shining the spotlight on us whether we wanted it or not. I'm pretty sure our notoriety was one of the factors that led to the death threats we received that September.

I accepted help from any direction. One unexpected ray of light came via Joe Ruggiero, a security guard I'd come to know through mutual business at the Sheriff's office. I liked him. He would accompany us on raids, and sometimes bring in useful information from the streets, anything just to be involved. Other police officers had looked down on him as a "wannabe," but I told them to lay off.

"He's a nice kid," I'd say. "Leave him alone."

One time in the early 70s, we'd run into a brick wall at nearby universities, where students seemed to be trying to incite unrest. We couldn't find the source of the disturbances, but we knew we'd find pushers at the epicenter, as many of the protesters were clearly high.

I asked Joe to keep his eyes open around the university. I'll never know who he had working undercover over there, but within a few days he gave me a list of students to watch. We set up surveillance and had our culprits almost immediately. Other officers started to look at him with a new respect. I'll never understand why he didn't pursue detective work; he certainly could have excelled there. I would come to value Joe's friendship even more a few years later, when everyone else abandoned me.

The never-diminishing line of drug dealers kept me working overtime most nights. Before and after every raid, I'd spend hours making sure I had all names correct, looking through every file for errors; it was a painstaking, time-consuming effort. I had to break often when my eyes started to hurt—I could stare at print for 15, maybe 20 minutes, tops. I didn't realize how many hours I spent at the Sheriff's office, or that my family was slipping away from me.

The death threats began after we arrested a small-time street dealer named Johnny Diaz the second time in three months. Duffy and I first arrested him in July 1972 for participating in an assault on a citizen that he and his buddies mistook for an undercover agent, and again on September 14, when we obtained a warrant to enter his home. We found about 6 pounds of marijuana there, and evidence that led us to another location where we seized an additional 35 pounds. Diaz was in some pretty hot water.

Rather than take responsibility for his mistakes and turn over a new leaf, Diaz decided that Duffy and I were the problem.

The first threats came the next day, almost as soon as he put up bail. We figured they were just crank calls. Over that weekend, undercover men received information that made us think maybe we should pay them a little more attention. The sheriff put nearly all of his deputies on the case.

Then a young lady named Nadine called to say she wanted to come speak to me about "something of grave importance." I figured it was drug related so I invited her to the station.

Nadine looked about 19, but seemed wise beyond her years. She dressed conservatively and clutched a small brown purse. I didn't recognize her, but she said she knew me because she had gone to grammar school with my daughter. When I asked her to sit, she perched on the edge of the chair and started talking immediately.

"Mr. Tuttolomondo, I think someone is planning to kill you." She leaned forward. "And another officer named Duffy."

I reached up and closed the office door, muting the din of station activity outside. Then, grabbing my notepad, I said, "I'm all ears."

Nadine explained that she'd been at a nightclub the evening before, waiting for a friend. She was a regular customer there, and thought nothing of it when another regular called Andy sat at the bar beside her.

"He says to me 'hey, don't you work for an insurance company?' and I told him I did." Nadine looked at the purse in her lap. "I thought he was about to hit on me."

"But he didn't." I tried to imagine why her job would matter.

"No. He just lit a cigarette and took a long drag, staring at me like he was trying to size me up. Just when I was getting annoyed, he asked how hard I thought it would be to get a home address for someone unlisted."

"Not hard at all, I imagine." I knew many companies that shared such data.

"Right. That's what I told him. Then he tells me he's trying to track down a Buffalo cop named Tuttolomondo."

I raised one eyebrow. "Did you tell him you knew me?"

"Not exactly." Nadine grinned. "I realized he was up to no good, so I kinda played along. I says to him, 'Why? You gonna' do something to the bastard?' He relaxed after that, as if we had a common enemy so I was safe to talk to, you know?"

I nodded. She wouldn't be safe for long if this Andy guy knew she'd come here.

"Then he told me a friend of his had a bone to pick with you. Said this friend is paying him a mint to take both of you out." Nadine pulled a slip of paper from her purse and slid it across my desk. "Then he gave me this and said he could pay me handsomely for my efforts."

I examined the phone number. I was pretty sure we could track it down. We later learned it was the number to a bar.

"I told him to let me see what I can find and I'd let him know."

"And what about the friend you went to see? Did he show?"

Nadine shook her head. "He might have, but I left right after that. That's when I called you."

Her concern seemed sincere; I believed her. *What did she have to gain by lying?*

"Did you find my address?"

She looked embarrassed. "I wanted to see if I could…"

"Did you find it?" I smiled. She met my grin and smiled back."

"It's right there in the phone book. Niagara County, not Erie. You live in Lockport!" Nadine would have made a great detective.

"Yep. They could have looked it up all along."

Nadine's story left me in an awkward position. While I was glad to have the information, there wasn't enough to warrant an arrest. Besides, her thug was small-time; I wanted the leader, the one with the vendetta. I was pretty sure it was Diaz. I thought I could catch him, but it would mean sending Nadine into harm's way.

"Young lady, would you consider meeting with Andy and wearing a wire so we can learn more?"

Nadine hesitated. "I'm not sure. What if he catches on?"

"We'll be right outside." I patted my shoulder holster. "Armed and ready to rush in. Plus, we'll give you a little training first."

She nodded slowly, biting her lower lip. I admired her courage.

Andy agreed to meet Nadine in a sleazy, noisy bar called The Dungeon two days later. We schooled her as best we could about what to expect, and we rehearsed a few potential scenarios. She was a quick learner—a smart cookie.

When I kissed Audrey good-bye the morning of the meeting, I noticed an unmarked police car parked outside our house. I knew another officer had been sent to Duffy's place to watch his family. I wouldn't return home for more than 72 hours.

One of our female deputies fixed Nadine up with a necklace-type listening device, hooking the bug under her clothes. You'd never know it was there. Amazing inventions, these little microphones—a police officer's friend. Taped corroborations had tipped many cases in our favor that could have ended in a stalemate of "their word against ours," particularly in bribery attempts. I've worn a device many times when someone was trying to bribe me; as soon as you present a taped conversation in court, the defendant's only option is to cop out for a lesser charge because he's *done*. The guy who set me up a few years later wasn't wearing a wire. He should have been. But if he had worn one, it would have helped *me*. He knew what he was doing.

The Dungeon thundered with activity that night. It must have been pay day, judging by the size of the crowd, but I don't remember. They had a live band that blasted rock and roll into the street. I sat with some deputies in a nearby van, wearing a headset so I could listen to every word.

In a surprise twist, Andy wasn't there when Nadine arrived, but my pal Diaz was, and he'd been waiting for her. Nadine played it cool and started to chat. She quickly realized she'd get nothing on the tape over all that noise, so she convinced him to step outside by saying she had the addresses he needed. All I wanted was to hear Diaz just *mention* the assassination plot and we could move in.

Wouldn't you know it; as soon as they walked out the door, some bozo came along and fired up his motorcycle not ten feet away. They raised their voices but the engine noise was just too loud. Then Diaz started looking around as if he were ready to go back inside.

I was pretty sure I'd heard enough of the conversation through the headset to make an arrest. Besides, I didn't want Nadine to be with him too long, or for him to leave the scene. We jumped out, put him in cuffs, and took him in for booking.

When we got to court, we played the tape, but the judge couldn't make out the conversation. We sent it to an engineer from California Technical Institute, who translated what he thought was the conversation, but the judge still couldn't make it out. We even sent the tape to a friend of mine at the FBI, where they took the background noise out. Regrettably, they still said the content was questionable.

It stung a bit to see Diaz set free. Still, he got the message. I stopped him on his way out of the courthouse and said, "I'll tell you right in front of your attorney, (once you arrest a guy you can't talk to him unless his attorney's present), if anything happens to my wife, I'll do you in. And if anything happens to me, I've got some good friends."

He knew I wasn't bluffing. I had a reputation by then as someone who makes good on a promise. Besides, he really was small time, and this episode most likely made him realize that murder plots were not his calling. I never heard from him again.

Back on the job, I nearly became disheartened by the worsening drug scene. Sometimes the guys and I wondered if we could possibly be making any difference. We had to be content with small victories. In 1973, we went undercover as employees at Bethlehem Steel, over on Furnham Boulevard. We not only arrested men selling drugs inside the plant, but we nabbed their supplier as well. We found a sizeable cache of cocaine, marijuana, and numerous types of pills at the supplier's apartment. It felt good to know these drugs were not going to get to their intended destination.

Well-groomed informants were becoming key players in our game plan. We spent a lot of time developing our informants and establishing trust in both directions before the relationships could bear fruit. As I had done with Giovanni, we initiated these relationships with small-time criminals upon their first arrests, offering to put in a good word with the DA's office in exchange for some information. If we told the DA's office we'd received assistance from an individual, they would sometimes lower or drop charges. Typically, after such assistance, an informant would bring us tips over time; consistent tips that developed into arrests would elevate his reliability ranking. It could take a long time for someone to reach "trustworthy" status, but it was well worth the effort. A good informant is worth about 500 hours of work to a police officer.

Mikey G had earned a place high on our roster.

In early 1975, Mikey G came to me about a guy named Skeeter, claiming he'd been responsible for a recent rash of drug store hold ups and drug deals. Skeeter had been stealing and selling Dilaudid, a powerful narcotic that was dangerous in the wrong hands. People were dying from Dilaudid in record numbers, but Skeeter had no qualms about selling it. He had no problem using guns during a hold-up either, and we considered him particularly dangerous.

Thanks to Mikey G's tips, we found and arrested Skeeter. The judge set his bail high—at least $100,000, if I remember correctly. We worked hard to build the case against him, both before and after his arrest. We knew we had an air-tight case when we searched his home and found a sawed-off .22 caliber rifle that had been identified by victims as being used in some of his crimes. He was going away for a long time.

I spent many meticulous hours filling out paperwork for Skeeter's case, tagging all evidence, and recording all statements with care. My eyes gave out occasionally, but I'd take a quick break, burying my face in my forearm until they were rested, then get right back to work. We turned everything over to the DA's office. The staff there then had 45 days to put together what should have been an open and shut conviction. After 45 days, the court considers the DA's office has demonstrated a "failure to prosecute," at which time they drop the case and release the suspect.

I hadn't been paying much attention to how much time passed, but you can be sure Mikey G knew. He called in a panic exactly 45 days later, saying "Skeeter is on the street, and he's looking for me! Tutt, I'm scared out of my wits!"

I gave Mickey G some of my own money so he could get out of town quickly. You had to protect your informants if you wanted to keep the others you had or acquire new ones. I called my DA's office, and learned that apparently the case paperwork had been mislaid and they hadn't even been working on it. Anger washed over me, and I completely lost my temper. I just screamed into the phone, spewing a long and ugly tirade of reprimand that I'm not proud of at all. The cleaned-up version of our conversation would have sounded something like this:

"This is *gross* ineptitude! Hundreds of man-hours, weeks of work, *wasted*! He was selling Dilaudid, for Pete's sake! We *had* him dead to rights! Instead, now I've got an informant on the run, fearing for his life!"

The DA's assistant responded with only a lethargic, "Sorry, Tutt, but these things happen."

I couldn't believe their lack of remorse. This was just another case for them. For those of us on the front lines, it had been epic.

After this episode, our squad's relationship with the DA's office deteriorated, and it was never the same. They had absolutely *nothing* to do with my set-up later that year; however, I'll always believe they pursued my arrest and conviction as far as they did because of our history—just a gut feeling—and I'll always wonder whether they would have tried harder to learn the truth if this incident hadn't occurred.

The Skeeter episode drained me. I'd put so much effort into that case that I could think of nothing else. I decided I had to get away, so Audrey and I started making plans to take a vacation.

I didn't know it at the time, but my marriage had been deteriorating much further that I could have imagined. In fact, I had a stronger relationship with the DA's office than I had with my wife. Audrey told me later that she had been on the verge of asking for a divorce. Even when I *was* home, I was no fun to live with. Joey had been asking me to go hunting, which we really enjoyed doing, but I kept putting him off. Our project time was waning; I just couldn't seem to make as much free time as I had earlier. He was 16 by then, and I was ignoring him at a critical time in his life. I told myself, that's just what happens to police officers' families.

In reality, I was so involved in my work, so stubborn, and so prideful that I justified putting family aside for what I thought was the greater good. The devil was feeding me and I was eating well: I'd become intoxicated by my life and the heroism that went with it. I didn't know at the time that Audrey and her parents were praying for me non-stop. Today I'll tell you the power of prayer cannot be underestimated, and I suspect those prayers were the catalyst for what happened next.

For our vacation, Audrey and I went to Thousand Islands, a quiet resort area on the U.S.-Canada border. I couldn't tell you many details, except that it was a beautiful place and I actually managed to leave my job behind and have some real conversations with Audrey. We spent a week taking boat rides on the Saint Lawrence River, visiting a few of the more than 1,800 islands in the region, and getting to know each other again. I'd forgotten how much I loved her. That week was just what our marriage needed.

With my personal life back on track again, I felt refreshed, revitalized, and ready to go back to work.

Little did I know, my law enforcement days were about to end.

A Kick to the Gut

September, 1975

It's easy to think you're in charge of your own life, until you aren't.

When I awoke on September 25, 1975, I knew all I needed to know about the world and my role in it: I knew my strengths and how to wield them, I could tell the difference between the good guys and the bad guys, I understood the legal boundaries of the justice system, and I knew who I could count on in a pinch.

By the end of that day, I was sure of nothing.

The day started simply. I'd been back from vacation for three days. I got up to speed quickly, resuming a case I'd set aside two weeks earlier with an attorney representing some boys from Depew, a small town just west of Buffalo that was seeing a spike in narcotics activity. Our undercover men had been running into walls trying to gain a foothold in the community, but it looked as if our luck was about to change. Just before I left on vacation, my old informant Giovanni (who had helped us break the City Hall hold-up case) contacted me on behalf of two Depew brothers who had been arrested for marijuana possession. I say contacted, but in reality, he walked right up to where I was sitting in a parked car, rapped on the window, and started chatting as if we were pals.

It had been years since I'd seen him; he was certainly no longer a frightened young man who would turn in a fellow criminal for a favorable word with the judge. Instead, he carried himself with a street-wise confidence that should have made me more cautious, but I wasn't going to turn down a chance to get into Depew.

Giovanni specifically wanted me to help the older of the two brothers, who claimed to have taken the blame for possession even though it was his brother's weed. I told him I'd pull the files and see what I could do.

Back at the Sheriff's department, I read their files and saw that the older brother had little to worry about—he'd probably not even serve time. I did put in a good word for him, and the DA's office did let him go, but I doubt my input had anything to do with it. The younger brother, though, he was in much more trouble; I thought he might be my gateway into Depew. If Giovanni would help me gain the young man's confidence, it might lead me to his suppliers.

I contacted Giovanni to see if he could get the young man to confess. "Make him tell us where he got his grass," I said. "Then we'll see."

I wouldn't say I trusted Giovanni, but he had come through for us before, so I wasn't overly suspicious. A short time later, the Depew boys' attorney, Leo Carlone, called me and said the boys were talking, but that I'd have to go through him for the information. When I headed off to Thousand Islands with Audrey, I promised Carlone I'd pick this case up as soon as I returned.

So, when I arrived at my office on September 25th, I had a good outlook for the day ahead, some money in my pocket, and a spring in my step. The money was already earmarked for tires, but it felt good to know I had it. It came from a settlement check I'd received from my father's estate—a whopping $678, which wasn't much but it was just in time because the tires on Joey's old Ford-350 were not going to pass inspection. I'd cashed the check a few days earlier, flashing a smile at the teller when she recommended I don't spend it all in one place. Although I'd already spent a little over $100, there was plenty left for tires.

And the spring in my step? I was going to meet Carlone that afternoon. He said he had a list of users and pushers that would guarantee I'd be in Depew making arrests in no time.

I'd asked for the names when he called, but he was uneasy providing them over the phone because someone might overhear.

He wouldn't consider mailing them, either. I thought he was acting somewhat over-paranoid for such a simple case, but I wanted those names. I asked him to come to our office in Buffalo, and I even offered to go to him.

"They're watching me," he said. "I can't do that."

I guess I should tell you, Carlone was himself a coke-head. I had a file on him, and I had information from a Federal agency that said he actually *was* being watched. This, in itself, was not enough to dismiss him as a potential source of information. However, it could account for some of his paranoia.

Finally, he agreed to meet me in a public place. He had an office downtown in Ellicott Square, so we decided to meet at a coffee counter in the lobby there. The day passed slowly; I felt like a kid waiting for a present, eager and excited.

I should have recognized the fear in Carlone when I saw him coming up the steps and I went out to meet him, but I attributed his behavior to drug use and possibly paranoia. Still, when he approached me and handed over an envelope, I pressed it first to make sure I wasn't being set up. I knew right away that it contained paper. An envelope filled with money has a certain hardness to it; any good police officer can tell the difference. I started to open it, but he said, "Don't do that here." So I put it in my pocket.

"I gotta run," he said, and he took off.

In seconds, the place was swarming with plain-clothes police officers. State police—guys I'd worked with, who knew me. They surrounded me and one officer pointed at my pocket and said, "Joe, what do you got there?"

I was shocked. The scene before me unfolded like a bad movie plot. I pulled out the envelope and held it out.

"It's a list of names," I said.

He said, "No, that's money," and grabbed it from me. I dared him to open it, but he wouldn't. I saw it on his face, that moment of realization as he pressed the package—he'd been duped.

I tried to piece it together later. The only thing I can think of is that Carlone must have gone to his District Attorney and said I was a bad cop, and that he was going to offer me a bribe. The DA probably gave him money and put it in an envelope, but Carlone must have had second thoughts, so he took the money out and replaced it with folded paper. That's what it felt like—folded paper.

So I've tried to see that moment from the eyes of the arresting officers, standing in a public area, having just arrested the chief of the Erie County Sheriff's Narcotics Bureau. The officer who took the envelope must have known immediately it wasn't money, so he didn't open it. Couldn't open it. He was afraid of a lawsuit, and there would have been one, I assure you.

For the record, I know the police officers at the scene were innocent, and they had been convinced somehow that I was not. I understand what was going on in their heads when they realized they'd made a mistake—they had to carry the scene to the end and hope it could all be fixed in the morning.

As far as I know, the envelope was never opened. It disappeared. I know that what the prosecution later offered in evidence as "the money" did not come from that envelope.

The prosecution claimed the envelope from Carlone contained $750 in marked bills. Who bribes someone with $750? That's less than a paycheck! I do believe that having $524 in my pocket didn't help my case, as it appeared that I was accustomed to walking around with large amounts of money. The state police later testified that my pocket money was in the form of five crisp $100-dollar bills with sequential serial numbers. My attorney had taken photos of the $524 (he photographed the three $100s and two $50s, but not the smaller bills). All my money was returned to me later that night.

My brain churned with anger and resentment, and with the need to profess my innocence. I offered to take a lie detector test and even take truth serum. They turned me down, saying it wasn't admissible in court. But I would have done it anyway. All I wanted at that moment was to clear my name.

Some officers escorted me to the District Attorney's office. The DA was an honest and honorable man—a former FBI agent. However, I believe he'd been sucked into the story, and that Carlone was using him as a pawn. He grilled me about so-called suspicious goings-on at the sheriff's department. I still wonder whether it was a coincidence that my boss happened to be at a Narcotics Enforcement Officers conference in St Louis the day this all went down. They must have known he'd be gone and figured that would make it easier to get to me.

The DA said, "You're going to Attica, Tutt. You're going to spend a lot of time there unless you tell me about your boss."

"What is there to tell?" I asked, "Do you want me to make something up like Carlone did?"

I had, and still have, no idea what he was talking about, or what he was searching for. He was trying to build a case against what he called, "that dirty sheriff and those rotten deputies," but I couldn't give him anything. Even if I *had* made something up, any story would have quickly fallen apart. My boss was an honest man.

Eventually the DA gave up.

"There's no use talking to you." He glared at me over his paperwork.

"I agree." I looked him straight in the eye.

"Get out of my office," he said. "You're going to Attica."

"So be it." I still believed we'd sort everything out.

At my arraignment later that evening, the DA recommended the judge set bail at $3,500, but my attorney convinced him to release me on my own recognizance.

I was charged with 36 counts, all felonies. That may sound like a lot, but a thorough arresting officer usually addresses every aspect of a crime to ensure the applicable charge is part of the list. That way, a criminal won't get off on a technicality. For example, someone who throws a rock through a window would be charged with throwing the rock, breaking the glass, trespassing, endangering lives with flying glass, and so on. Thirty-six counts was just a sign of diligence. By the time the dust settled, only two charges remained: That I had solicited and accepted $750 from Leo Carlone, and that I had demonstrated conduct unbecoming of an officer. The punishment for bribery was up to seven years in prison.

The most difficult part of that whole ordeal was returning home. Duffy drove me because I had driven to work in a sheriff's car. I'd turned over the keys with my badge and gun. Audrey had heard I'd been arrested, but thought it was part of an undercover operation. She met me at the door, stepping aside to let me in. I could see the questions in her eyes. Duffy didn't even get out of the car, leaving me alone to explain to her what I didn't understand myself.

We went to bed but stayed awake all night. Audrey was convinced that everything would be set right in the morning. She'd seen me get into some unusual situations, although getting arrested was something new. She believed whole heartedly that the men I worked with every day would fight to get to the truth of the matter.

Audrey's confidence was so resolute that the next morning she got up and went to work. By then, the story had hit the streets; it was all over the news on television and in the morning papers. The hospital staff was surprised to see her, but she told them she planned to go on as if nothing had happened and let my friends in the department take care of me.

They did not. Men I'd trained, shared life and death moments with, put my trust in, were suddenly afraid. Even Duffy. That's what happens when someone on the force is arrested. Nobody will associate with him for fear of being drawn into the case. I knew what they were thinking: *If the chief can go down, imagine what could happen to me, a mere lieutenant, a captain, an ordinary detective!* I held no bad feelings toward them at any point in this unfolding.

Nor do I have bad feelings toward Carlone, believe it or not. Of course, I did at the time, but my view of the ordeal has changed. We found out later that he'd been snorting coke like crazy at the time. He was a user *and* a dealer, which made him doubly dangerous. I know he set me up, but I'll never know why; perhaps he had goings-on in Depew and I was getting too close. It no longer matters.

Regardless of motive, someone devised a perfectly orchestrated plan, and it was carried out flawlessly. Looking back today, I'm grateful for every piece of the puzzle, but that gratefulness didn't come right away.

Encounter on the Lane

October, 1975

For ten days after my arrest, thoughts of hatred and revenge consumed my every waking moment. Not only had those brutes attacked me, my reputation, my nearly 20-year career, and my pension, but as I fumed I convinced myself that it was much larger than that: they were attacking my wife, my son, and my entire family. A small part of me felt grateful that Pa and John were gone; I was sure that if Pa had been alive, the shame would have destroyed him.

But my other siblings knew. Jenny knew. I wondered if she understood...if she believed. And the others? I knew my siblings' loved me, but would they believe me or what they read in the papers? The news media was having a swell time covering the story. One paper even revisited the incident with Ralph when I'd been in Vice, clearly recounting that my gun "accidently fired and killed a suspect," but not including the details that I'd been absolved of wrongdoing, or that I could have been killed.

I passed the days stewing in my misery, alternating for hours on end between angry tirades and sullen reflection. I replayed every detail of the arrest, searching for missed clues. Audrey tip-toed around the house. Whenever she came too near I'd start venting where I left off. "Why didn't he open the envelope? He knew! He must have known!" Or, "I've arrested people for bribery before. You wear a wire for that! Why didn't he wear a wire?"

It must have been hard on Audrey, listening to me rant and being unable to help. I hurtled a lot of anger around that place. I yelled at her, and at Joey, because there was nobody else around. Audrey cried herself to sleep every night. I know she prayed fervently, as did her parents and our friends from church. A couple of times she tried to show me a scripture she'd found that day, remarking about how timely it was. Once she showed me a line from the book of Proverbs that said, "A false witness shall be punished, and whoever pours out lies will perish." I could only sneer. If that were true, then why was I being persecuted?

I did not pray. I couldn't waste my time on such nonsense; I thought if I could just figure this out, I could fix everything by myself.

My most dangerous thoughts were about how I was going to exact revenge on Carlone. Whatever I did to this guy I could easily justify. He had it coming.

On the tenth day after my arrest, a plan for revenge began to come into focus. I grabbed a jacket and headed out the back door to think, walking along the grassy lane that led to Audrey's parents' home. The newly harvested corn field flanked one side of the road, and a hay field ran along the other—a lovely farm scene, but its serenity was lost on me; the autumn leaves in the distance may as well have been dirt for all I saw. My heart seethed with hatred.

I'm going to kill Carlone.

If I'd learned anything in my years as a police officer, it was what factors to consider in devising the perfect crime. I could snuff out that liar without leaving a shred of evidence. Sure, everyone would suspect me, but they couldn't prove a thing without evidence. My scheme had to be flawless; to the last detail.

Make no mistakes, Tutt. You're in enough trouble.

I'd have to act under cover of darkness—make it easier to create doubt if it came to court and someone testified that they'd seen me.

"Saw, or *thought* you saw?" I could ask.

I couldn't use a gun because the noise would carry for blocks; noise carries farther at night.

I couldn't use my bare hands (although I was certainly capable), because he might shout and draw attention.

Then I had it: a bow and arrow—perfect!

A swift and quiet death.

As an accomplished archer, I had years of hunting pheasants and other game under my belt. He wouldn't know what hit him. Of course, I would have to make the arrow by hand because a commercial one could be traced. I couldn't take any chances that might be traced back to me...

Right about that time, a single word interrupted my train of thought. I tried to push it away, but it came back again...and again, subtly at first, but with increasing intensity.

Jesus.

I couldn't make it stop. Sometimes a word, sometimes an idea. It was quite frustrating. I thought, "Stop this religious foolishness and get serious!"

Jesus.

Little did I realize that during all those services I'd sat through, while I struggled to stay awake, I'd been subconsciously learning the message of the Bible. And now here I was, at the crossroads of my plans and God's plans, and all the sermons were coming back. I found myself thinking, *this is not what Jesus wants for me.*

With hindsight, I can tell you that a *lot* of people were praying for me at that exact moment—Audrey, my in-laws, and all those Christian people I'd thought were so nice and goody-goody, but foolish. They were praying hard, and their prayers were working.

There it was again. *Jesus.*

I burst into tears, right there on the lane. I'm not one to cry easily. In fact, the last time I'd cried was when John died. But there I was, sobbing uncontrollably. I knew Jesus was there with me, listening to my scheming, watching me lower myself to the level of those who were persecuting me. I knew I was letting him down. Shame engulfed me like a tidal wave, nearly crushing me beneath its weight.

I sank to the ground, broken and afraid, and I prayed.

"Lord, I don't want to be like they are!" I could barely recognize my own voice. "Please forgive me! Oh God, I'm such a sinner! Come into my heart, into my soul, into my life. Show me what to do. I can't do this by myself!"

I'm not entirely sure where those words came from—they were so out of my character—but I knew I had to say them. The only way to describe what happened next is to say that every bit of hatred left me in a flash and I felt the huge crushing weight being lifted.

In its place, an unexplainable joy washed over me, making my problems miniscule compared to what had just happened. I knew peace—real peace—for the first time in my life.

With an uncanny realization, I understood that my arrest, the upcoming trial, and even its outcome were all part of God's plan, and would somehow answer everyone's prayers. How that could even be *possible*, I had no clue, but I knew I had to trust that it was.

Most surprising, I lost all desire to kill Carlone, or to hurt him in any way. My anger toward him changed to genuine concern for his soul, and a hope that one day I could talk to him about Jesus.

It boggled my mind that I really felt that.

Other changes started occurring in me at that moment, most of which I realized over time. For instance, I had been a champion curser, but from that day forward I never swore again. And all those Sunday school lessons I dozed through, the readings and sermons, now every word made sense. In an instant, I had become a new person.

I lay there a while longer, not wanting the moment to end. Then restlessness overtook me, and I desperately needed to tell someone what had happened. Anyone. I rose and brushed the pebbles and grass off my clothes. Glenn and Ruth's house was just ahead of me, where Audrey had gone for lunch.

I raced up the lane and met Ruth coming out of the house. A strange mix of surprise and curiosity registered on her face.

"Joe, what happened?"

"I've accepted the Lord!" I grinned so wide, my face hurt.

She nodded, unfazed.

"I can see that." She smiled. "You're just glowing."

This is where my testimony really begins.

On Trial

1976-1977

A Bible verse in Paul's Letter to the Philippians describes "a peace that passes all understanding." I never gave that verse much thought until my experience on the lane, yet it's really the only way to explain my state of mind in the face of what most people would consider absolute tragedy. Throughout the next 15 months, while the prosecution compiled evidence and tried its case against me, I experienced a near-constant state of peace. It made no sense, particularly since I'd acquired a lengthy list of reasons to be angry.

To begin with, I'd been publicly humiliated. Regardless of the trial's outcome, there would always be people who thought I was guilty. They were reading every news story about my case with a gleeful certainty that I was heading down in flames.

My career was certainly over and I'd lost my pension, ten months shy of retirement eligibility. Every day I was going deeper into debt paying legal bills, but I couldn't even get a paper route with the arrest hanging over my head.

Our professional friends were dropping us one-by-one. Men I'd worked with for years, who had trusted me with their lives, were now distancing themselves. I understood that they couldn't put their own careers at risk by associating with me, but it hurt anyway.

Audrey was also dealing with humiliation, although most of her coworkers were supportive. At first, they joked that it must be a ruse for another undercover assignment. They'd become accustomed to seeing stories of my escapades in the news. Only one coworker said outright that she thought I was guilty.

Joey's once-admirable grades suffered greatly, to the point that we worried he might not graduate his senior year. He'd always been a good student, but the upheaval in our home as well as the ridicule he endured at school made it hard to focus on his work.

Despite all this, we were happier than we'd ever been, and I was experiencing the most serene peace a person could know. These were difficult days, without a doubt, but today Audrey and I look back on them with thanksgiving, and honestly say that was one of the best years of our marriage.

The foundation of my peace came from reading the Bible. Now that I understood that my life was in God's hands, I earnestly wanted to learn everything I could about him. Someone described the Bible as a letter from God to me, so I poured over it each day as long as my eyes could stand it, laughing at how I'd scoffed at Audrey's Bible back when we were dating. For the first time, I was actually reading and understanding the words, and putting the pieces together.

I attended Sunday services at CMA, *my church* now, with an entirely new attitude. I no longer dozed through the sermons or challenged the teachers. I was hungry, and hung on every word. Nearly every day I found something—a verse, a story, an example to aspire to—that helped me cope with that day's events. And the hymns and psalms, what beautiful poetry! They explained emotions my heart couldn't put into words and taught me how to worship, and I mean *really* worship the Lord.

All this learning didn't ease the seriousness of what I was going through, but it did show me that there was more to my suffering than what I could understand from a human perspective. I realized that God saw a greater picture, and he was orchestrating events all around me, even if it didn't make sense from where I stood.

In the midst of all the drama, I was not the only family member in trouble. We were all concerned about Jenny, who'd been having some abdominal problems. She went to the clinic, where they told her she had gas. Then it got worse, and her belly began to swell. She went back thinking she was pregnant, but the doctors still insisted it was gas. Turns out she had an ovarian tumor that was cancerous and inoperable.

Learning this almost broke me. My father had told me to take care of Jenny in event of his death, and here I was, nearly helpless. I visited her as often as possible. I'm not sure she fully understood what was going on with me, but I was more concerned that she knew who Jesus is. I asked her nearly every time we met.

"Jenny, do you know what it means to accept the Lord into your heart?"

"Sure." Her brown eyes would laugh at me. "I go to church. I go to communion. I understand."

But I knew she didn't.

I could no longer slip Jenny money because I had none. Fortunately, Casper, Sam, and Jo still lived nearby. I knew they would look after her if I had to leave.

The finest lawyer I knew represented me: Jonathan Prescott, a man I'd come to admire and respect over our years of interaction. A veteran who fought in the Normandy invasion of WWII, he was a tough, but prevalent and sought-after defense attorney who had represented many of the people I'd arrested over the years. Up to that point he'd never lost a case. He knew my reputation as a hard-nosed cop and that I did not bend the law. He also believed my story, for which I was very grateful.

Yes, Jonathan was the best; he was also quite expensive. Even after exhausting all our savings, I went nearly $60,000 in debt over legal bills. We sold the toys in the barn: the ski mobiles, the carriage, the sleigh, and then the horses. As the trial approached, I also had to part with the Alpha Romero. Broke my heart, but it had to be done. As the possibility of going to prison became more likely, I signed the car over to Audrey, figuring that if she needed money she could sell it. She had to sell it almost immediately. Compared to everything else I was losing—my job, my reputation, my freedom— it was a minor thing, but it was big to me. Joey and I had a lot of good memories tied up in that car.

Some of our greatest moral support came from members of our CMA congregation, who quickly filled the void left by my law enforcement "friends." They visited often, fixed us meals (although we didn't ask for them), welcomed us with open arms every Sunday, and, most importantly, formed a support team to pray for us throughout the ordeal.

Of all those I'd worked with in law-enforcement over the years, only my security guard friend, Joe Ruggiero, stood by me. Just days after my arrest, he came to the house and asked how he could help. I immediately thought of Carlone.

Interestingly, the official files I'd been keeping on Carlone disappeared the night of my arrest, and Jonathan could find no record against him. I couldn't tell Jonathan or Joe what I knew, since the Feds hadn't completed their case yet, but that didn't mean Joe couldn't start from scratch.

"Do you suppose you can get anything on Carlone?" (Sure, I trusted God, but I thought perhaps he could use some help.)

Joe didn't hesitate. "Let me put my sister on it."

Joe's sister was gorgeous from head to toe. She had a lovely face, exotic brown eyes, long, dark satin hair, and a figure that made men stare. She agreed to go to a bar that Carlone frequented and see if she could catch his attention. Did I mention she was gorgeous? It didn't take long before he approached her with an offer to hook her up with cocaine and bring her into his fold. She relayed all this info to me and Jonathan, so we had dirt on him that we could add to my recollection from the missing files, but the judge deemed it all inadmissible. She couldn't testify against Carlone because he wasn't on trial, so it didn't matter. I still appreciated Joe and his sister for their efforts.

My trial at the State Supreme Court began in mid-November 1976. The trial lasted five weeks, and I could fill pages here with a moment-by-moment recap, but that's not what this book is about. I'm not concerned about proclaiming my innocence, but describing the journey, so I'll only mention the highlights. In short, the case against me was well-prepared and served its purpose: to put me behind bars.

I first realized how high the odds had been stacked against me when I learned which judge would hear my case. During my nearly 20-year career, whether as a police officer testifying after an arrest I had made, or as an undercover cop requesting a search warrant to topple a drug ring, I had met just about every judge in the system. I'd watched them all come up through the ranks from City Court, to County Court, and on to Supreme Court. And they all knew and trusted me; I thought at least I had that on my side.

Instead, my case was heard before the only judge in the county that I'd *never* met. His reputation as a tough judge preceded him; he was a man of honor who despised the idea of "dirty" cops.

During the trial, Carlone testified that he'd been planning to have me arrested for bribery, but said he hadn't worn a wire on the day of the bust because the tape hurt his chest. More likely, he worried I might let on that I'd been expecting a list of names. Regardless, instead of a wiretap, he arranged for police officers to hide in the shadows.

Jonathan tried to present an audio tape of my pre-meeting phone conversation with Carlone. The tape clearly conveyed my insistence that Carlone come to the office or that he mail me the names, as well as his claim that he was being followed. It could have established innocence, but the judge deemed it inadmissible and would not allow the tape to be played for the jury. Instead they read from a typed transcription "in context," which, I believe, must be a fancy term for "important information omitted." In a later appeal, Jonathan fought to obtain the entire conversation, and at one point the prosecution agreed to provide it, but it never appeared.

Giovanni testified that, not only had I taken this bribe, but he had also paid me off two other times, to the tune of $3,500. I found out later that police had nabbed him a few days after my arrest with a lot of money on his person. Without skipping a beat, he claimed it had been for me. They quickly offered him witness protection to testify against me. He told the jury that he had given me some money the day before my arrest, in hundred-dollar bills. I think the DA believed Giovanni's testimony only because of what Carlone had said, and that's what turned the DA against me.

Giovanni had an arrest record as long as my arm. The jury didn't want to hear from him. The prosecutors sensed that and dropped him, but the damage had been done. The jury apparently put a lot of stock in our 10-years-past relationship from the City Hall holdup days, so parts of his story sounded plausible.

The prosecution speculated aloud that the amount in my pockets upon my arrest must have come from the previous day's "take," despite testimony from the bank teller that she had cashed my father's estate check. She had copies of the check and could prove I had taken it out of the bank. Her testimony became lost in a confusing debate over bill denominations, serial numbers, how much I had in my wallet that night, and how much was in the envelope. One uniformed trooper even testified that he'd found five $100 bills on me with serial numbers that matched those recorded before my arrest. They would not accept the photograph of my wallet contents as evidence, which would have refuted his testimony.

The news media was no help. They seemed to embellish every negative aspect of the trial to slant the story against me wherever possible. Audrey and I would come home at night and read the account of that day's proceedings with amazement. We could only look at each other and say, "Were we *at* that trial?"

My own testimony lasted 80 minutes. I was calm and polite, and answered as best as anyone could when questions are phrased like allegations. I told the same story I've laid out on these pages. However, the prosecution had done its job well and had neatly tied up all the elements needed for a conviction. As an experienced police officer who had trained others how to build a concrete case, I knew how it would go, but it was difficult to watch the testimony play out. I'd try to talk about something and they'd stop me. I couldn't tell them my side of the story. I was frustrated that certain things were allowed and others weren't. As the questioning continued, the stack of cards against me grew.

Despite the odds though, I remained optimistic. When I prayed, I felt a sense of peace that made me think everything would be okay. I placed all my faith in this peace, believing that God had orchestrated all these events long before I met Carlone on those steps.

The jury deliberated my fate behind closed doors for three days while I waited outside the courtroom. The seven-woman and five-man jury returned twice to review testimony. Once, they wanted to examine the written phone recording of my call with Carlone; the court still allowed only that someone read them the transcripts. The voice inflections and foul language weren't there, just a monotonous drone of, "Mr. Carlone said this, and then Mr. Tuttolomondo said that."

I'm sure that if the jury could have heard the desperation in Carlone's voice begging me to meet him, they might have come to a different conclusion.

So I sat outside the court room every day because I needed to be available when they called us back in. Audrey and I spent the time in prayer, reading the Bible, and counting our blessings. I kept telling Audrey, "Don't worry, God has a plan."

Of course, then I'd look up and say silently, "You do, don't you?"

To my great relief, all my drama wasn't going to ruin Joey's chances of graduating. Although he was still struggling, it looked as if he would make it. On the down side, he was going to have to attend the local community college because we had just relinquished the last of his college funds to pay Jonathan.

Audrey plied me with Bible verses and prayed with me for a favorable outcome. By then, I'd become a great advocate of prayer, and of the power that can come from trusting God. The trial had been tough, and it was looking as if truth had lost, but I found peace in knowing I was right where God wanted me to be. I also knew that somehow, I wasn't going through this for nothing. Truth can be hidden, but it cannot be changed. I knew the truth.

The peace must have been evident on my face, because people kept asking me how I could be so composed when there was so much at stake. When I'd tell them I was leaving it in God's hands they'd just shake their heads and walk away. Late on the third day of my long wait, a Jewish lawyer who knew me passed by and had to stop to ask, "How can you just sit there so calmly? If it were me, I'd be crawling up the wall."

I said to him, "I'm surprised, Aaron. Jesus was one of your *paisans*. You really should learn more about him." He lowered his head and shook it, clearly thinking I'd lost my mind.

That was the difficult part about my new peace. People could see it in me, and they'd ask about it, and I wanted to tell them, but I had to suppress it at times because I realized they didn't really want to hear the answer. A surprising number of people, even Christians, thought it was either an act or I was going nuts.

Finally the jury returned. It was December 15, 1976. I knew the guard who led them into the court room. When he walked past me I said, "I hear they've reached a verdict."

He turned and looked me straight in the eye and said, "Yeah Tutt, they have."

That was all I needed. I could read it on his face. I'd been found guilty.

The judge's gavel came down; I was now a convicted felon. I felt disappointed. No, more than that. Shocked. I'd honestly thought I'd be acquitted.

How could they not recognize all the perjury that had taken place?

One reporter later quoted me as saying repeatedly, "I just don't believe it."

Well, I didn't.

Regardless of what happened from this point forward, my police career was over. I thought back to those first days in the Police Academy, when I'd vowed to leave the force with my head held high. I felt a surge of pride to know that I could still do that. It didn't matter what those around me thought, I and the Lord knew I had served honorably.

My former coworkers had no choice but to handcuff me for the trip to the Erie County jail. They showed respect by cuffing my hands in front instead of behind my back, and they asked if I wanted to say goodbye to Audrey. With the cuffs in front, at least Audrey and I could hold hands. Seeing those tears run down her sweet face pierced my heart.

"Don't worry," I said to her, "I'm in good hands. The Lord will take care of me."

I'm sure she thought I was putting up a brave front, but I honestly believed it.

Jonathan arranged bail, but unfortunately, such things take time. I wound up spending the night in that familiar place—a place where I'd personally locked up many of Erie County's lowliest characters. I had trouble believing it was happening to me.

Audrey's mother drove her back to our house. She told me later that our pastor, Robert Burton (or Pastor Bob), had been waiting there when they arrived, as were many friends and family members. They stayed for a few hours, until the phone rang and it was me, telling her I was fine. She said I actually sounded happy.

The guards smuggled me into the jail through a tunnel to avoid the media gaggle out front. Part of me had to laugh, because they were taking me to my own jail and my own guards were going to guard me. I received no preferential treatment because I was still a hot potato and they were afraid to be too nice to me.

Alone in my cell, I began a lengthy discussion with God, voicing my frustration with his decision. I said, "Okay Lord, I'm a Christian now. I understand why you made me go through all this. I was so proud and arrogant; I had to be knocked down to see you. This all brought me to you and has strengthened my faith. I deserved it and I'll always be grateful. But I don't understand why I still have to go to prison."

As I prayed, my eye caught the white edge of a small piece of paper on the floor. A remnant of a Bible tract, which is a devotional leaflet Christians bring when they visit prisoners. I picked it up and read the words aloud, *"I will never leave you or forsake you."* I had read that in the Bible a few days earlier, so I recognized it. The remainder of the verse came to me in a flash: Hebrews 13:6, *"So we say with confidence, 'The Lord is my helper; I will not be afraid. What can mere mortals do to me?'"*

I thought of my mother, telling me about the dog that dropped his bone to get the larger one in the water and lost both. I took great comfort, both with the realization that as a Christian I could now be sure I'd see her again, and in knowing this was God's way of telling me I was right where He wanted me to be.

Be content with what you have, Joe. You have so much.

There it was again, that peace.

I laid my head down and was just about to fall asleep when a guard I knew well came to my cell and said, "Gee Tutt, I'm really sorry to hear about what happened."

Then he just sat down and started to talk. He had a lot on his mind. I listened because it's all I could do. He talked about the shaky relationship he had with his wife, and said that his wife had left him and was on her way to California with the kids. Tears were streaming down his face and he sobbed, "It's over."

"Nah, it's not over," I said. "Regardless of how bleak things are now, they will get better. Think of how bad things look for me, and yet, I'm as happy as a bug!"

He said he couldn't believe that, but I told him how the Lord had been working in my life, and that I really was at peace with what was happening. I encouraged him to try talking to God for himself.

"You can BS me, and you can BS yourself," I said, "but you can't BS God. "You've got to be on the level with Him. Try it. See what happens."

I had to laugh again. Here I was, convicted of two felonies and sitting in jail, telling a free man how to be happy. We shook hands and he left, and I haven't seen him since. I'll never know if he took my advice, unless we meet in Heaven.

It had been a long day. I closed my eyes and slept soundly for the rest of the night.

We made bail the next morning by putting the house up as bond; I was free until the judge called me back for sentencing, which could be months.

Jonathan immediately filed for appeal. Regrettably though, I'd come to the point where he and I would have to part ways. Although there were still many hurdles ahead of us, I simply couldn't afford him any longer. Audrey and I had prayed about our finances, but the money had run out. I met him in his office that evening with a speech prepared.

"Jonathan," I slid into my usual chair across from his desk. "I'm so grateful for everything you've done. But I don't think we can continue. Our money has all run out, and Audrey and I have borrowed from everyone we know."

"I figured as much." Jonathan opened a desk file and pulled out a sheaf of papers. "Here. Read this and sign it."

It was an agreement to pay Jonathan in installments, $50 per month until the debt was gone. The printed total was significantly lower than I'd expected it to be.

"But this doesn't account for—"

"I know, Joe." He folded his arms across his chest. "The rest is *pro bono*. Whatever you need."

My heart nearly burst as I took in this news. That caliber of attorney just doesn't work for nothing, yet here he was, laying all profit aside for me. I went home amazed and humbled.

Money being the most pressing issue, I went to Licata's Pizza Place down the street from our home and asked for a job. Joey had worked there through his senior year and the owners, Fran and Charley, knew us well. They treated me like family and said they'd be glad to have me. Working brought back memories of days in the kitchen with my mother, and I enjoyed myself there. The job kept my mind occupied and provided some sorely needed income; as little as it was, every penny helped.

Joey enrolled in the local community college. During one of his first weeks there, a professor who was teaching about government corruption said to my son, "Mr. Tutt, you have experience in that area, would you like to expound?"

He was a big guy by then, and Joey could have done some damage if he'd wanted to. Instead, he calmly stood up, gathered his things, and walked out of the classroom, never to return. I am still proud of that. I would have punched the guy out.

Joey went to live with his mother in Wisconsin, where he established residence and was accepted at the University of Wisconsin on probation.

With broken hearts, Audrey and I watched Joey leave. I felt doubly distraught knowing this meant Audrey would be alone when I went to prison. Still, we all agreed it was for the best. He'd have a clean start at school, and he'd be safe. We didn't know what kind of worms might have been let out of the can during my investigation, so getting him away from Buffalo was a good thing. Joey did well at the university. He had to load box cars all summer long to pay the tuition, but he kept his grades up. He even made the dean's list a couple of times.

The long wait for sentencing also gave me a chance to put my affairs in order. I talked to my in-laws, whom I now called Mother and Dad, about the upcoming property taxes. They graciously agreed to pay the bill. I then made up a budget for Audrey so she could live on her nursing income while I was gone. A man from the IRS came knocking at my door to audit my taxes; if I was getting all this money, they wanted to see what I was doing with it and whether I'd paid taxes on it. I not only let him look at the year just past, but asked him to check the two years before that as well. I said I had a feeling I'm going to prison and I wanted to be sure my wife doesn't have to deal with this while I'm gone.

After a thorough review, the auditor determined my taxes would be "accepted as filed" and that no further audit would be warranted. I asked if he'd heard about my trial, and he had. I asked if he'd ever heard the investigators ask about my finances, or check it out; he said no. I said, "I would have done that, wouldn't you?" He said he would have.

A local reporter I knew and respected named Lee Coppola asked me for an interview. When I'd been on the force, he had covered many of our arrests, always giving an honest account without embellishing the stories. I said I'd give him an interview and answer every question he asked, but he'd have to print everything I told him. He agreed.

I gave my testimony and, true to his word, he printed every bit of it. I told him about my being saved on the lane and becoming born again; about how much I'd hated Carlone up until that point, and how the hatred had just dissipated; about the strength I received from the Lord and that I felt I owed those who "destroyed" me a debt of gratitude because they had actually saved me. He wrote down every word and got the story past the city desk. The reporter, the editor, and everyone else involved paved the way for my story to print...that doesn't happen in most news rooms. My redemption story was plastered on the front page of the second section on March 2, 1977, on the same day my sentencing was announced on Page One. After that, nearly every article about me included a statement about my faith.

Coppola's article also sparked a letter-to-the-editor debate as to whether my salvation came too late. People were reading about and discussing Christ right there in the daily papers. One man wrote a lengthy diatribe saying I shouldn't have been given space in the paper for such a disclosure, not understanding that God was using him to keep the topic going. The director of Buffalo's Police Community services had the last word in *that* argument with a succinct letter that said, "Obviously, whoever wrote this is not aware that it is never too late to diligently seek Him, nor of the depth of Christ's love."

Coppola's story took some of the sting out of that horrible day and my experience before the judge during the sentencing. At first, I still thought I might get a lighter sentence. Then again, until that day, I'd had no idea how much the judge despised me.

Before he sentenced me, the judge asked if I had anything to say. I had prepared a statement so I stood up. I said, "I've spent 20 years building a career. During those years I've been shot at, stabbed, beaten, and hospitalized. I gave so much of myself that I deprived my family of myself and I was deprived of them. We will live the rest of our lives under the stigma of this case, compounded by the fact that I did not commit this crime."

I looked the judge in the eye. "Sir, I ask that you please consider the many people I put in prison who are still there. If you sentence me to prison, you'll be sentencing me to death."

However, the judge had been hardened. "We have here a police officer who feathered his own nest in an insidious way, extorting money from others." He addressed the courtroom but his eyes were fixed on me.

"Perhaps, Mr. Tuttolomondo, while you're in prison you will meet up with some of those people who haven't been able to pay your extortionist fees and they will settle up."

Audrey burst into tears behind me. No sentence could have made me sorrier than I was at that moment, knowing the pain she was going through.

He chastised me further for attacking Carlone's honor on the witness stand.

"That's unforgivable," he seethed. "You tried to brand an honest attorney as a felon and you the victim. I'm going to take that into consideration." Then he sentenced me to up to seven years in prison.

Jonathan's repeated attempts for appeal put off my sentence for another eight months. I asked him once why he worked so hard when my case was pretty much sewn up. He said to me, "I've never known anyone like you. There's a goodness about you."

"It's not me," I said, "It's what I've become."

"Yeah, I've read about it," he answered. That's all the explanation I ever received. He was truly a decent man.

Everyone gets one chance at the appellate court, during which a panel of judges examines the case and the proceedings to determine whether there's any reason to readdress the findings. Well, they looked at my case and decided to keep things the way they were. The two-year fight was over. My last appeal was denied on November 14, 1977; the time had come to report and to begin serving my sentence.

To be honest, I was ready to go. I needed to put all this behind me. As I left the courthouse, again in handcuffs, the media swarmed. There had been a lot of speculation in the papers as to my chances of surviving in prison with prisoners I'd help put behind bars, and the likelihood of finding a prison where there *wasn't* someone who knew me (not likely at all). Amid the shouting reporters I heard many questions, but one stood out.

"Joe, are you scared?"

I stopped in my tracks. I just had to answer that one. A quote from Paul's letter to the Romans flashed across my mind like a neon sign. I waited until the crowd settled before I spoke.

"No, I'm not scared at all. All things happen for the good for those who love the Lord. You may not understand that until you've accepted Jesus. I've accepted Him."

Then, right there in front of the cameras, I bowed my head and prayed. The media plastered pictures of me praying on the front pages of every local paper that day, along with my quote from Romans and words of hope. I'll probably never know what God accomplished through all of that, but I'm still glad to have been of service.

After spending another night at the Erie County Jail, I transferred to Attica late the next afternoon. I saw myself on the evening news as we entered the building. Inmates were standing around the television, watching me say I wasn't afraid and listening to me pray, while behind them, I was heading toward my cell.

Prison

November, 1977

We've arrived back at the start of this story. I'm in Attica, in protective custody among murderers, thieves, and drug dealers, all of whom consider *me* to be the lowliest sort of despicable criminal: a narcotics officer with a tarnished badge.

I'm prisoner 77C633. A sparrow in a cage surrounded by 2,000 hungry cats. Two guards are posted not ten feet from my cell, protecting me from "the population," and I'm staring down at a folded piece of paper that says, of all things, *"Stay encouraged."*

To be honest, those were the last words I'd expected to read in that place. I'd been prepared for the worst. My first thoughts when that paper soared into my cell had been, *"and so it begins."*

Yet that scrap of paper, ripped from a spiral notebook and tossed covertly into my cell, turned out to be a ray of light and a precious gift. I forgot the prisoners who were parading past on their way to supper, laughing, jeering, and jostling with one other, and staring at me through the bars. Turning the paper over in my hands, I unfolded it to reveal neatly penned words of hope:

> *"Mr. Tuttolomondo, I also am saved. I accepted Christ in my life last year but unfortunately I still had cases pending, so here I am. But thanks be to God I'm as free as a dove because I can know wherever I am, Christ*

is there also, and there's a blessing in this for me and for you, so keep your faith no matter what people say or do and stay encouraged because we have overcome the world. God bless you, your brother in Christ, Harl. Rom 16:20."

By then I was familiar with the book of Romans. The verse Harl included came from Paul's closing words to the fledgling Christians in Rome, in which he wrote, *"The God of peace will soon crush Satan under your feet. The grace of our Lord Jesus be with you."*

I was astounded. In my concern about the enemies I'd meet in prison, I hadn't even considered I might find allies. I looked at the cement ceiling and prayed a blessing over the man who had written the note, thanksgiving for the encouragement, and, almost as an afterthought, I asked for forgiveness for any doubt I'd been harboring.

"I'm new at this, Lord," I said. "I do trust you, really."

As if in answer, a second note came flipping through the bars, this one tossed by a Hispanic inmate who grinned and flashed me a peace sign as he disappeared around the corner. I snatched up the note and again smiled upward in thanks before I read:

"Hi, my name is George, otherwise known as Joe. I've read every article concerning your case, and I could just imagine your situation, and how you feel, personally. I am also a person who thinks 'Martian,' [Christian] and I sympathize for you and your family, regardless of who or what you were. Because of this experience you will be a better man, and from this note you will also realize that there are some human beings in jail capable of sentiment for others no matter what, who and where. I wish you the best of luck on your appeal and other matters. I just had to let you know how I feel after seeing you walk the yard. Your friend, Joe. Cell 15."

And, because I've learned that God likes to show off sometimes, a third note soared into my cell as the last group of inmates returned from chow that night. The messenger was a tall, noble-looking Indian, who looked directly into my eyes as he flicked the folded paper. Staring back at him, I knew I was looking at dignity, quiet strength, and inner peace…real manhood. I opened his note and read it:

> *"Joe, Excuse the informality, but under the present conditions, we are equal while under the wing of the Department of Correctional Services. I, too, am from Buffalo, and like yourself, feel that I shouldn't be here. As a man whose past stature [is] such as yours, I must commend you (if I'm in a position to) on the way you are taking what's being given to you. My purpose for writing this note is to encourage you to keep your head high and to have faith in your God as I do in my Great Spirit. Hang in there, A. Friend."*

I stared through the bars at the wall across the now empty corridor for hours, considering these men. For the first time, I understood that we were all the same in here, regardless of skin color, background, or the alleged criminal offenses that brought us here. Some were guilty; others were not. Some were repentant; others would repeat their crimes in an instant, given the chance. It didn't matter. We all had two things in common. We had our minds, which could not be imprisoned, and we had time—all the time in the world. These mattered.

I resolved to devote my time and my mind to living for the Lord. At the moment, I didn't quite know what that meant. I was already seeing proof that my actions were being watched by others. Although I'd only heard from believers thus far, I was sure many nonbelievers were watching me as well.

When the guard delivered my food that evening he asked if he could get me anything. (Incidentally, the guards at Attica were professional and respectful. I'm sorry to say I was surprised. I'd heard so many stories about this place that I'd expected harsh treatment.)

"Yes," I said. "I could use a Bible if you've got one."

He returned with a New American Standard. I'm a King James man, but I was happy to have anything. I began reading, starting with the Psalms and went through the first 22 before the day ended. Pastor Bob visited a day or so later. He brought me a King James Bible that I still have today.

I would spend only a few days in Attica, and all of that in solitude. Attica was merely a processing station, as it was close to Buffalo. Had I remained there, I'm sure I would have located those three men and learned their stories. I thought of them often, however, and I prayed for each of them. I prayed most earnestly for the Indian, because I knew he understood God as a spirit but I wanted more for him.

At one point, I thought back to that long-ago day at a Buffalo park, and that "scumbag" professor who had approached me for sex. I understood him now. Sure, he was wrong, but he wasn't bad. The two words are not the same. I wondered if he were in a prison somewhere, I wished I'd known to pray with him instead of judge him so quickly. We were all the same in God's eyes...all sinners, and all in need of a savior.

Three times a day the inmates trekked past my cell, alone and in pairs, to get their meals. There were no escorts because guards controlled the cell doors remotely, cycling through the blocks until everyone had eaten and returned "home." I glimpsed my letter writers once or twice, but we never talked.

Within days of my arrival I quit smoking for good. It was easy because I no longer felt the need for stress relief. Prison represented the beginning of the end. Every day I spent there brought me one day closer to returning to Audrey and putting this saga behind us.

Naturally, I filled the cigarette void with calories; the food there wasn't bad at all, and my tall, lean frame filled out rapidly. I hoped for some sort of regular activity in my future.

One week later, I received transfer papers to the Clinton Correctional Institution in Dannemora, which is as far upstate New York as one can go, near the Vermont border. Nearly all New York prisoners are channeled through Clinton, where they wait while a review board examines their records. The board determines the most appropriate prison for each person based on his crime, criminal history, and required level of protection. I knew placing me would present a few problems, considering my need for additional protection.

"Up to seven years" meant I would serve at least 18 months but no more than seven years. I prepared myself to do the full seven. I could only hope to leave any earlier if I confessed my "crime" to the parole board, and there was no chance of that. However, I also knew that if I kept myself out of trouble I could apply for a furlough after a year, as well as a work release permit. Either of these could make prison life a bit more bearable.

I left Attica wearing a green prisoners' uniform that made me look like an appliance repairman. I boarded the prison bus, noting that all the inmates had their hands cuffed and their feet shackled to each other so they couldn't run. There must have been some police officers in the brotherhood who believed my story, because they cuffed only my hands and didn't shackle me to the other prisoners.

During the more than seven-hour drive to Dannemora, my mind began to unravel. Despite the beauty of the Adirondack Mountains outside my window, I could think only of home.

I thought about Audrey getting further and further away. It made my heart sink. I thought about how she would be adapting to life as a single woman again; and about my sister Jenny, who needed me; and how I'd promised Dad I'd take care of her, and here I was letting him down because I couldn't even visit her. I thought about my brothers, Casper and Sam, and my sister Jo, wondering whether this had cost me their respect. It was foolish thinking, I know, because they had each sent me letters of encouragement, but that's where my mind took me during the long drive north.

That first night in Clinton was probably the worst night of my entire sentence. Anxiety set in the moment that cell door clanged shut. The horrific stench of musty, dank basement and body odor hit me immediately; I still cringe when I think of it. My teeth chattered incessantly because it was so cold. Inmates yelled nonstop, at me, at each other, and at nobody in particular.

Someone had used either a cigar or cigarette to burn the word, "Remember" onto the concrete over my bed. There's a lot to say in that one word, and I think I dwelt on it a bit longer than I should have.

I felt my blood start to rise and an overwhelming sense of anguish come over me as the reality of my situation sank in. I honestly thought I was about to break. I tried to pray, but couldn't retrieve any of the assurance I'd felt in Attica. The idea that I was alone, the indignation at being unable to clear my name, the trial, the losses, my son's move to Wisconsin, picturing him saying to his new friends, "my father's in prison." It all caught up to me at once and I found myself lamenting that my life was over.

With hindsight, I now know that God tends to do His best work in our moments of weakness. Accordingly, He chose that moment to give me the boost I needed, through Audrey. I had advised her earlier not to write until I was settled and could give her mailing instructions. True to her style, she ignored the logic of my instructions and wrote anyway, hoping her letter would reach the prison when I did. When the guard passed her letter through the bars, I was floored that it found me. To my further amazement, she'd written the exact words I needed to read at that moment. She quoted from 2 Timothy, which says, "*God did not give us the spirit of fear but of power, and of love, and a sound mind.*"

I suddenly felt as if she were there, and Jesus as well. The anxiety left me in an instant, and I reaffirmed my Attica vow to put my mind and my time to good use. Opening the King James I'd acquired from Pastor Bob, I turned to Genesis and started to read. The darkness, the cold, and the noises subsided as I focused on the fascinating and powerful stories of Israel's founding fathers. Day after day I read, stopping only to eat, sleep, and write letters home.

Almost from the first day I noticed that my eyes were no longer watering from strain. My eyes had been so bad for my entire life that the change was not only noticeable, it was undeniable. I reckoned it must be either God or the mold, as I was fully immersed in both.

Okay, I was pretty sure it wasn't the mold.

Meals marked the passage of time. If it weren't for breakfast, I wouldn't have known when night became day. If not for dinner, I wouldn't know another day was nearly over. I could take one short, tepid shower a week.

Clinton's protective custody area consisted of a row of damp, windowless, sub-basement cells. They were so cold that after one night I thought I'd *never* be warm again. Trying to focus on the positive, I told myself that at least it cut down on the odor. I couldn't imagine what it must have smelled like there during the summer.

Still, cold was my biggest enemy in those early days. I wore everything I owned all the time (jacket, two shirts, two pairs of trousers, two pairs of underwear—all of it), and I stayed wrapped in my blanket. It didn't help that all I could see in the corridor outside my cell was a radiator—a constant, taunting reminder that there *was* heat here, just not in the cells. Every 23 hours they'd open the doors to give us an hour of "exercise," but instead of moving around, we'd all make a beeline for the radiators and cluster around them. We cherished what heat we could soak up during that hour.

We didn't talk during radiator time. I was amused at the incredible discrepancy between the men's conduct behind bars and then out in the open. At night the inmates taunted, argued with, and threatened one another up and down the row of cells. They had no idea who they were yelling at, but curses and retorts would fly back and forth for hours. Then, the moment the cell doors opened for exercise, everyone stepped out quietly. I witnessed very little eye-contact, and no bravado.

What little talking we did was guarded. You never told your crime. If someone asked, "Waddya in for," I'd say "Manslaughter." I'd tell them I was in a bar and some guy started getting friendly with my wife so I hit him and he died. If they asked why I was in protective custody, I'd answer, "He has relatives here."

This type of self-preservation came naturally to me. I was new to Christ, but *Omèrta* had been so prominent in my upbringing, I relied on deception in the face of perceived danger. However, as I read more of the Bible, I began to realize that I was supposed to tell the truth in all situations and let the Lord handle any reactions. It was a difficult transition for me, but I knew in my gut it was the right thing to do. After that, I never volunteered information, but I didn't lie either.

From the front of my cell (or, as I'd started calling it, my cage), I talked about Jesus to anyone who would listen. My audience was sparse, consisting primarily of the inmates on either side of me. I couldn't see them, and they never replied, but I talked anyway.

I called the man on my left Mohammad, although I never learned his name. I knew he was a Muslim because he called out to Allah every night during shouting time. He refused to come to the radiators when the doors opened, even on the coldest days. He said Allah wouldn't want him to associate with us "blue-eyed devils," and demanded that his cell door remain locked.

Then, as night settled in, I'd whisper around the corner, "Jesus can save you. He saved me. Jesus is here with us."

He did not respond. Not once. Yet, in the middle of the night I'd hear him cry softly to Jesus, and ask Jesus to help him. I prayed He would, but I never learned whether our prayers were answered. (That's *another* man I'm going to have to ask about when I get to Heaven.)

I could now read for hours on end with no vision trouble; I read the entire Bible in just over a week. When I reached the end of The Book of Revelation, I flipped the pages back to Genesis and started again. Much of it still didn't make sense to me, but on the second time through, a lot more became clear. I processed much of what I was learning in my letters to Audrey. She said she believed the Holy Spirit was teaching me.

I'd just settled into the Book of Exodus one Friday when I heard keys rattling at my cage.

"You have a visitor, Tutt." A correctional officer (we called them all CO) opened the door and stepped back to let me out.

Probably one of the many counselors I've seen this week.

I turned out onto the walkway and fell in step behind two guards. Behind me, my liberator and another guard closed the ranks.

Four on one. Now *that's* security.

Instead of entering a counseling room, we turned into the visiting area, a large open space filled with heavily guarded tables. Around the tables I saw faces from all walks of life, and nearly every emotion imaginable—peace, sorrow, hope, remorse, frustration. I wondered what they all found to talk about.

But we passed all these tables and stopped at a table in front of two COs. That's when I saw my beautiful Audrey, sitting expectantly with her parents. They looked so out of place in this land of tough guys, I couldn't help but laugh.

We'd been apart nearly a month, but it felt like years. I wanted so much to sweep her up, but I slid onto the seat beside her and just started praising the Lord for bringing her to me. Of course, I snuck in a few kisses, but the guards looked the other way.

Ruth opened a small bag of oatmeal raisin cookies that she'd made, not knowing they were forbidden. (Raisins could be used to make alcohol. I often wondered how many cookies I'd have to pulverize to get enough raisins for a good swig.) However, since this was our first visit, the guards were kind and let her bring them to me. I guess they knew I wouldn't be brewing in my little cage.

We talked about everything, and about nothing. Audrey rattled off messages from well-wishers back home, and brought me up to date on family matters. Throughout the discussion, I caught her staring at me often, as if trying to determine whether I was right in the head. Finally I couldn't stand it any longer.

"What's wrong, Audrey?"

"You've changed." She searched my face as if looking for clues. "Can you really be this happy, or is this an act you're putting on to get yourself through?

I smiled. "Most of my joy comes from being able to see my lovely wife. But yes, I am completely at peace with what's happening."

Audrey and her parents stayed in a nearby hotel that weekend. They came back to visit Saturday, and then again on Sunday to say good-bye. The entire weekend was such a joyful surprise that I still grin when I think of it.

Sadly, as much as I enjoyed seeing them, I had to discourage further visits for a while because Buffalo may as well be Miami when compared to Dannemora's harsh winters. Here it was only the second week in December and we'd already received 30 inches of snow, and the temperature was averaging 20° below zero. I couldn't stand the idea that any of them would become stranded in a snowdrift just so I could get a kiss.

I wrote to Audrey almost daily, which posed a minor issue because I was limited to five out-going letters a week and my friends and family were inundating me with letters and cards that I wanted to respond to. We devised a system; I'd include two or three letters with each one of hers. She'd repackage and mail them on to the rightful recipients. Occasionally I'd write a blanket letter to everyone that she would type up, photocopy, and send out in the mail. Many of them found their way into CMA church bulletins on Sunday mornings.

After a second week at Clinton, when I'd read through the Bible a second time, I announced that I was ready to leave protective custody and become part of the "population." I had to sign a waiver saying I understood the risks. I did, and I accepted them. I knew how quickly an incident could occur. I'd heard stories of how a group of four-to-six guys would form around someone holding a knife or a shank. Then they'd pass by their target and the guy would just drop, yet apparently, nobody ever knew who did it.

In light of such incidents, the prison officials changed my status to "Close Monitoring Case," or CMC, which meant they had to know where I was at every moment. My prison counselor said that being a CMC pretty much guaranteed I'd never be granted a furlough or work release. Apparently, people who committed violent crimes were granted furloughs, but not Organized Crime members or ex-cops. I said we'd see about that. I was beginning to catch on that God truly enjoyed responding to the word "never."

Because of my CMC status, I was placed in what was known as a limited population area, a large, dormitory-type area that housed about 20 inmates and had a very small yard. I could walk the yard, but I had to go alone. Even in the winter it was a blessing to be able to get out.

One afternoon as I was heading back from the showers I met up with Chiefy, my old "buddy" from the East Side drug ring. Of course I recognized him; he hadn't changed much in ten years, except perhaps to become more ornery looking. I could tell by the cluster of inmates who walked with him that Chiefy was well respected in the prison community, and that he was well protected. I'd have to walk past him to get to my cell area.

I wasn't afraid. Too many things had happened in the past few months for me to ever really be afraid again. However, I was wary. After all, he'd held a knife to my chest once before.

Holding my head high and staring straight ahead, I walked past the group of inmates. In my peripheral vision I scanned the inmates' hands, checking for signs they might be concealing something. It was a bit anticlimactic, because I passed right by without incident.

Reaching the other side, I exhaled and started to pick up my pace, but I was stopped short by Chiefy's familiar baritone.

"Hey, Tutt!"

I turned and looked him in the eye, saying nothing.

"I just want you to know...I followed your trial." He shook his head slowly. "That wasn't right, what they did to you."

He turned and went to the showers, leaving me standing there with my mouth open.

As soon as the prison officials realized Chiefy had recognized me, they moved my cot next to the guard's desk and a guard brought me my meals from that day forward. The incident not only highlighted the guards' professionalism and quick reaction, but it also expedited my permanent assignment paperwork. Clearly, the guards wanted me out of there.

I received my assignment a day or so later, on December 9, 1977. As it turned out, I wouldn't be leaving Clinton at all. Instead, I'd be assigned to a work crew that stayed in an annex building right there on the prison grounds. My counselor said I would be spending the days outside and only come inside each evening to sleep.

I could barely contain my joy. Sure, I would have preferred a prison closer to home like Albion, but I'd known such an assignment was unlikely. The prospect of having physical work was exciting, considering how much weight I'd gained between inactivity and dropping the smokes. And besides, I absolutely *hated* doing nothing (and still do to this day).

A short time later, I had all my belongings wrapped in a prison shirt and I was escorted outside the walls of the main building to the medium-security farm compound. The Annex was an old, two-story converted hospital building that had upper and lower rooms on one side and a row of windows on the other, with a guard station in the center of the first floor. I'd heard from other prisoners that it was a great place to serve out your sentence. If you had to be incarcerated, they said, you couldn't do better than the Clinton Annex.

I entered the building to a scene that was anything but peaceful. An inmate stood at the guard station, yelling at the correctional officer in Italian and gesturing wildly with his arms. His words were music to my Sicilian ears. The CO, however, had no idea what he was saying and was trying helplessly to calm the man. As I listened, it became apparent that, like me, the inmate had recently transferred to the Annex, but that some of his personal belongs had not arrived.

"He needs his stuff," I said to the CO. "Especially his address book, so he can write to his friends and family. It's still back at the main building."

The inmate was so happy, he kissed me! Then he started rattling off details as I translated, telling the guard where the items were located. The much relieved CO wrote down the information and said he would look into it. All missing belongings arrived the next morning.

The inmate's name was Mario. Thrilled that he now had someone who could help him communicate, he put his arms around me and let everyone know he was my friend. Mario was in prison for homicide, which meant his social standing was high. It also meant the protection he afforded me was invaluable.

How do you like that? I'm there not ten minutes and I already had a friend with prestige!

My good fortune continued. I couldn't believe the palace that was my room! The Annex was medium security, with real rooms instead of cells. Such a contrast to the tiny cage I'd lived in "behind The Wall," as inmates referred to the main building. I could stretch in any direction without smacking concrete or bars. I even had a beautiful window with *clear glass* (it's amazing what you learn to appreciate once you've gone without), as well as a locker and bookshelves.

I scrubbed the whole place down with disinfectant, shined the chrome fixtures, and set my things up the way I wanted them. The room reminded me of military officers' quarters: kind-a-neat, as Joey would have said.

Of course, there was a catch. The doors to our rooms were never locked, except when we left for work. The guards had access to our rooms whenever we were in them, even at night while we slept. This went so far against the grain of my personality that at first I could not sleep at all. The possibility that someone out there was waiting for an opportunity to kill me was quite real. My sixth sense was on overdrive as I lay there, waiting for someone to enter my room, while my mind raced through various self-defense options. Finally, I could stand it no longer. I got out of bed to fashion a burglar alarm.

I tied a piece of thread around the door knob and strung it across the room, to an aluminum can I'd placed on a shelf. I connected the thread to the can loosely with a paperclip that I had shaped into an "S." If someone pushed open the door, the thread would disconnect and the can would fall to the concrete floor. The noise would wake me and I could defend myself. It was a fool-proof alarm. I settled back into my bed, but I still couldn't sleep. Instead, the Bible story of Peter walking on water played across my mind like a dream.

I pictured Peter stepping out of the boat, reassured by his Master's gaze. He had every reason to trust Jesus, and had witnessed many events that should have removed all doubt as to Jesus' ability to protect him. But then, although he was already walking on water, Peter took his eyes off Jesus, letting fear and doubt take over, and started sinking into the sea.

Watching this story unfold, I came to the frightening realization that I, too, had taken my eyes off Jesus, and that I was sinking. The words from Proverbs 3:5 that I'd read a few days earlier flashed like a neon sign before me. "Trust in the Lord with all your heart and lean not on your own understanding."

So I rose, disarmed the alarm, and then returned to bed. This time I slept soundly, as I did every night after that. I knew I was again experiencing the peace that passes all understanding. I figured the

Lord could keep me alive if that was God's will, and nobody out there was going to take my life if it wasn't His plan.

Living at the Annex was quite different from the cage. No more once-a-week, 5-minute showers; I could shower twice a day if I wanted to, and for as long as I liked. And, although the farm complex had its own mess hall, the Annex had a common area with a fridge and a stove, in case we wanted to cook, and a color television in a sitting room so we could just hang out. There was also a gym and a recreation room. I didn't yet understand that the Annex inmates had established a hierarchy that determined just who hung out and when, so when I looked at my new home, I could only be pleased.

I didn't have a work assignment yet, but I knew I would be either a road worker, a grounds keeper, or a farm hand, as those were the only opportunities for people living on our floor in the Annex. Kitchen workers, maintenance men, commissary and building workers, janitors, and barbers lived upstairs. All totaled, about 130 of us lived there.

At first only Mario, my new Sicilian friend, would talk to me. Each night inmates gathered in the common area to chat and share foods they'd received from home. I was not invited to these gatherings. Mario may have had prestige, but he was not one of the leaders. Only the leaders extended invitations.

Mario, now that he could talk to someone, was only too happy to teach me the ropes. He helped me understand the Annex hierarchy and unwritten rules I'd be expected to follow. First, just about everyone there belonged to a gang, and I use that word only because that's what the groups were called. They were nothing like the stereotype associated with the word "gang" that we see on our city streets. Inmates would spend the day with their respective work units, which were made up of mixed races, but at night they'd settle primarily with their own group.

We had three main gangs, each led by a tough, menacing looking warrior. Although the groups intermingled, there was no doubt where their loyalties lie.

Topio led the Hispanic Gang. He was loud and energetic, but mean. Most of his men were Puerto Ricans who bonded tightly. I could understand a little Spanish, but not nearly enough to keep up with their constant chatter. One of their particularly explosive members was a scrappy Puerto Rican named Jacko, who was easily riled and so ready to fight about anything that most men stayed away from him just to avoid trouble by association.

King was the head of the Black Gang. He was a strong, quiet, but imposing figure. I saw in his eyes a wise man with worldly experience, but one who wouldn't be crossed. I hoped I never would cross him. I recognized one of the men in his gang right away—Kuba, a man I'd arrested about three years prior. We did not acknowledge each other, nor did we let anyone know we recognized each other. Deep down, I think it's because we knew we had a good thing here in the Annex, and there's no telling which of us would have been moved if we spoke up.

An Italian named Big John led the White Gang. Big John was tough and had a menacing leer that could make any man back down. He had high status at Clinton because he was in for first-degree robbery, meaning he'd been armed. His mere presence commanded respect, and I could tell even Mario feared him.

I did not intend to join a gang. I kept to myself, reading scripture and writing letters. When we went to meals, I prayed over my food before I ate, making no attempt to hide my faith. Glancing up, I'd see glares of disdain as well as approving nods. I returned both with a smile.

I wrote a lot of letters. Now that I had a locker, I wrote to Audrey telling her my new address and asked if she would send two packages. We were allowed two food packages each month that could weigh no more than 35-pounds combined. We could also receive separate packages of clothing and other non-food items.

For the food box, I requested peanuts, licorice, beef jerky, and some of Mother's delicious cookies (without raisins). For the other I requested a good padlock with 2 keys, some pencils, a hair dryer, and a turtleneck sweater (*not wool*, but a hand-washable material, and in the acceptable color range—no blue or black allowed).

As word spread about my arrival, inmates started approaching me with questions about my faith. This came as a surprise to me at first, but then I learned that my prison nickname was "Holy Man." I realized that although I'd earned this title when the media ran so many photos and stories of me professing my faith, I perpetuated the role by never being shy or ashamed to pray in public or discuss my beliefs. I had to laugh because it came so naturally. After all God had done for me, I was *compelled* to talk about him. It struck me at one point that most of the inmates had never heard the name of Jesus except in a string of curse words. When I prayed in the evenings, I told God I hoped we could change that.

Topio was the first of the inmate leadership to talk to me. He assumed because I read so much that I was well educated, and he came to me for help filing his appeal. I was glad to help, and we spent a few hours one evening at a table in the common area drafting his letter. He couldn't do enough for me after that, and with his seal of approval, I knew I had nothing to fear from his gang.

Fellow Christians introduced themselves to me, and invited me to attend Sunday service and other events. Some gave me inspirational books and other literature, which I eagerly devoured and then passed on others. One day a man who said he was a Quaker chatted with me for a while and then handed me three books, among them *Prison to Praise* by Chaplain Merlin A. Carothers. When I opened it, my eyes fell on a verse from Thessalonians 5 that said, *"Rejoice evermore, pray without ceasing, in everything give thanks, for this is the will of God in Christ Jesus concerning you."* I felt it was addressed specifically to me. I knew God had me right where He wanted me, and I could only be grateful.

I read all three books quickly and appreciated the wisdom they contained immensely, but I still treasured my daily Bible reading above everything else. I was beginning to realize that the Bible message changes continuously, depending on the reader's situation. Of course, the words are the same, but one's attention is drawn to different details as his own needs change. As such, the Bible was an evolving source of comfort and instruction whenever I was facing a difficult situation.

For example, at this point in my imprisonment, I understood that God had put me in prison to teach me to rely only on Him. I was sure I had responded as He'd wanted, so why was I still here? I'd been reading in my Bible about young David, the boy God anointed to be future king of Israel. His story resonated with me. David would have to wait *years* before he took the throne, and I admired the faith he displayed even though the current King, Saul, was trying to kill him. David would have been content to learn from Saul for many years. Instead, because of Saul's hatred, the boy was forced into hiding in the hills and caves, unjustly accused of treason and fighting to survive. Rather than lose heart, he continued to voice support for the king, even when the opportunity to kill him presented itself. David could have easily taken matters into his own hands, but he knew it wasn't the right thing to do. Instead, David settled his parents in a safe haven with the king of Moab, asking the king to protect them, "Till I know what God will do for me."

I could understand David's anguish, as well as his response. Like David, I didn't understand why I was in my situation, but I wasn't consumed by the idea of vindication. Instead, I trusted in a plan I couldn't see, and I determined to be content to wait there, 'til I knew what God will do for me.

In mid-December I was told to report to the correctional officer on duty for my work assignment. He grinned as he handed over my clothing issue: long johns, flannel shirts, a sweater, a hooded parka, and overshoes. Something told me I wasn't going to Bermuda.

"Welcome to Little Siberia," he said. "Looks like you're going to be a dairy farmer."

I completely missed the cold reference as I tried to imagine working on a farm. Tossing hay, milking cows, breathing that fresh mountain air; it all sounded so wonderful, I giggled like a child at Christmas!

I went to bed early that night…farmers get up before the sun.

The Farm

December, 1977

Little Siberia. That guard wasn't kidding. Folks up here were fond of saying that Clinton has only two seasons: Winter and July, and I wholeheartedly agreed. Although I wore nearly every bit of clothing in my Farmer Joe issue, I never felt truly warm. It didn't matter. I was outside, and I was working. After living in the cage, this was heaven.

As I pondered my assignment to the Clinton Annex, and to the farm rather than a road crew, I realized that every turn in this saga brought about events that shouldn't happen to me; conversely, nothing that *should* have happened to a former narc in prison ever happened to me. I was never attacked, sabotaged, shunned, or bullied. All I can say is, this must be what God's grace and provision look like.

There's no way I should have been placed on the farm. For one thing, I was brand new to the prison system. Most inmates assigned to the Annex had already served time behind The Wall at the main prison for at least a year (many for much longer) and were nearing the end of their sentences. In theory, because they knew a good deal when they had one, these inmates were less of a flight risk. Perhaps that's why I went there: these men were also less likely to harass an ex-cop. It worked in Kuba's case, anyway.

I and two other new dairy farmers started our first day on the crew with an early morning driving tour of the snow-covered grounds, escorted by corrections officers, of course. The farm manager, Mr. Williams, drove the truck, while his assistant, Mr. Kovitch (inmates rarely learned the officers' first names) pointed out the milking barn, the chicken coop, pig sty, some maintenance shacks, and a small office, as well as an entire field that was reserved for Tino, the Herford bull. The dairy had been donated to the prison by a local farmer many years earlier. The farm's approximately 150 cows produced all the milk and other dairy products consumed at the prison, with enough left over to provide some to other area prisons as well.

We drove about a mile or so northwest of the prison to the perimeter of the property, where the officers let us stand a few moments to gaze at the incredible view. I was mesmerized by the peace that emanated from the valley below us. The endless blue sky was like a canopy over the snow-covered foothills of Dannemora Mountain, and in the distance, past the clear blue expanse of Lake Champlain, I could make out Vermont's Green Mountain, also draped in white. Despite the bare branches on most of the trees, the scene took my breath away.

"Right over that hill there is New York State Route 374," Williams said, shifting a wad of chew in his cheek. "It's an easy hike if you want to try it. Just know that we'll find you, and once we do, we'll add time to your sentence for escaping. Not only that, but you'll be sent back behind The Wall for good.

As if on cue, the three of us shifted our gaze south to the far-off dismal gray walls of the main prison, and the Annex complex nearby, each representing entirely different lifestyles. I looked back and was surprised to see Mr. Kovitch scowling at me. Did he know me? He certainly didn't look familiar.

Mr. Williams spit a brown stream high over the fence and flashed us a wide, tobacco-stained grin before adding, "You should also know that we don't mind at all if you try to run. We get overtime for chasing you."

No shackles exist that could have restrained us more effectively than those ten minutes on the hillside. Mr. Williams had nothing to worry about, and he knew it.

My first jobs on the farm were shoveling manure and washing cows. Many would consider this to be unpleasant work, but I grinned continually, grateful for every minute of it. Not only did I have something to do, but I got paid—not much mind you, only pennies a day, but everything helps.

Almost from the first day, I called the cows my ladies, and I endeavored to learn all I could about them. Despite my brief years in the rural town of Lockport, I was still a city boy, fascinated by the entire operation. These simple, giant beasts were so mild-mannered and full of God's provision, I loved being around them, and I shoveled manure as if their lives depended on it. In no time at all, Mr. Kovitch promoted me to feeding the cows.

I was puzzled by Mr. Kovitch. I could tell he appreciated the way I worked, however, he rarely spoke around me, and when he did speak, something in his face still registered suspicion. I didn't think it my place to question him, so I just kept my head down and did what I was told. If he had something to say, he'd have to come to me.

Many mornings began with a trek through freshly fallen snow. Plows cleared the way to the farm entrance, but not to the barns beyond. Because you can't *not* milk the cows, we had no choice but to blaze a trail. A different inmate took the lead each day and the rest of us would follow closely behind, trying to step in the footprints. On stormy days, the trail would be gone when we started back to the Annex in the evening and we'd have to create it all over again. In blizzard conditions, we'd each put a hand on the shoulder of the man in front of us and fight our way forward, heads down. But you know what? We were still so glad not to be behind The Wall that we didn't complain. Well, not much.

I stayed busy all the time, but I liked it. I became so acclimatized to the extreme cold that I'd overheat when I came back inside. In my room at the Annex, the radiator system had a seven-foot pipe running floor-to-ceiling; I always turned it off. It didn't occur to me that there might be some poor soul in the room above me who couldn't get any heat.

About the only down-side to the job was the smell. A dairy farm smells like manure. Everyone knew when we were heading back to the Annex because the odor arrived first. We came in, hung up our clothes and hit the showers.

Life settled into a routine. We'd get up at 5 every morning, dress, and jump on the truck so we could tend to the morning milking before breakfast. We'd work all day, stopping only for meals, and then head back to the Annex after a 13- or 14-hour shift. I still spent most of my evening time alone, or chatting with Mario in the TV room. I hadn't yet been invited to nightly snack time.

The packages I'd requested from Audrey came quickly, and contained all I'd asked for, as well as much more. There were pictures of her and the kids, which I quickly hung on The Wall beside my bed, and foods Audrey knew I missed. As I stocked my locker, I was overwhelmed with gratitude for both the gifts and for such a wonderful wife.

I didn't know that, once again, the Lord was working through Audrey to help me adjust.

While I was admiring a beautiful Old World Italian pepperoni stick she had sent and getting ready to stow it, Big John stopped at the door to my room and just stared. I could tell by the longing in his eyes, he clearly hadn't had authentic pepperoni in a long while.

"Hey Tutt," he said at last, "why don't you bring that out tonight." I nodded, and saluted with it, unable to speak.

Unsure whether I was being summoned in acceptance or for some sort of hazing, I said a quick prayer for protection before following Big John to the common area, and I asked the Lord to lead our conversation. For good measure, I reached back into my locker and pulled out a can of *capolitina*, a traditional Italian mix of tomatoes, eggplant, olives, and capers. If something as simple as pepperoni made his mouth water, *capolitina* would blow his Italian mind.

Turns out I had nothing to fear. Big John sat beside me and offered up some sardines and crackers from his own stash, and he took my offerings in a display of genuine appreciation. In this breaking of bread, he was saying to the rest of the prisoners that I was accepted. He was also establishing leadership over me. I had no problem being under his protection, but I would not express loyalty to him or any of the other leaders. I followed only one leader.

Fortunately for me, no such pledge was requested. We sat there with ten or so other inmates for about an hour. Most of the conversation was about things we missed back home, and about people on the road crew, which was Big John's work group. I thought he was nice enough, aside from a brief tirade during which he banged his fist on the table to cut off an inmate who was trying to speak and shouted, "Don't interrupt me when I'm talking!" The poor inmate cowered in the corner for the rest of the night.

Big John talked readily about the other gangs too, occasionally describing various inmates with racial judgments and stereotypes. I wondered if he knew any of them. He clearly trusted none of them.

I, on the other hand, was developing relationships with inmates at a rapid pace. I didn't know why, but it may have been because I tried to treat everyone the way I wanted to be treated. This proved to be particularly helpful when I was paired with Jacko—easily the most despised person in our building, and particularly on the farm. Everyone was wary around him, not necessarily because he might hurt them during one of his outbursts, but for the trouble they may get into around him. The looming wall of the main prison nearby served as a constant reminder of what happened to fighters.

One afternoon I was working with Jacko and Nash, a new inmate on the farm. Jacko was weighing the milk for each cow and calling out numbers while Nash and I recorded the data. (If a cow was a big producer, she got more vitamins and grain. If she didn't produce enough milk, she was no longer worth the grain and she'd be put to slaughter.) I'd adjusted to Jacko's heavily accented mumbling, but Nash was completely lost. Finally, after Nash asked, "What was that?" one too many times, Jacko snapped. He stormed up to Nash with fire burning in his eyes, pointed at me and shouted, "Holy Man here don't hear too good but even he's better than you! What's your problem? You got a problem with me?"

Nash didn't know how to respond. He looked at the ground and then up at me, with panic in his eyes.

I knew that if I yelled, the situation would escalate, so I decided to do the opposite.

"Jacko." I mustered a calm I didn't quite feel. "Do me a favor, would you? I need you to stop yelling."

The transformation was uncanny. Jacko stared at me for almost a minute, processing some far off data. Then he slowly, and *clearly* said to Nash, "Because of this nice man, I say I'm sorry."

Inmates who had come running at the sound of yelling about fell over in shock. From that day on, Jacko worked hard to keep his temper in check, and had fewer and fewer outbursts. For some reason, he also decided I was his friend. I was floored that my simple request had made any impact, but there must have been much more going on during that processing minute than any of us could ever understand. After that, whenever he could, Jacko would work next to me.

"You nice man, Mr. Tutt," he said often.

I'd tell him, it's not me, it's Jesus. He didn't quite grasp it, but I prayed he would. In one of my letters home, I asked our congregation to pray for him as well.

As I adjusted to my life in the Annex, I was heartened to find so many avenues available for Christian worship and fellowship. Aside from Sunday morning church services, and Sunday afternoons of contemporary prayer and singing, there were Wednesday night Bible studies. I quickly learned that it wasn't enough to just read the Bible, but there was another whole layer of understanding in knowing how all the pieces fit together. So many of the stories were related to each other, and some of the books even made predictions that came to pass thousands of years later. Every week it seemed I learned something new or connected a few more dots, and an "aha!" light bulb would flare in my brain. I practically *felt* my faith increasing.

A 7th Day Adventist preacher led the Bible studies; his views were different from mine, but he clearly loved the Lord. Some nights I interrupted with questions, and I'd bring up scripture that conflicted with his points. (After reading straight through twice, I could recall a lot of Bible verses, just because it was still fresh in my mind.) I was still quite the novice in Biblical theory, but I figured I should speak up and represent opposing views where people's faith might be influenced. It made for some lively discussions, and I do believe those who attended were given plenty to think about as they made up their minds.

One evening, as Bible study was wrapping up, the inmate sitting beside me asked if I planned to attend the CIA meeting the next night. I only knew one entity with that acronym, so I'm sure the look I gave him was less than brilliant.

"What's that?"

"It stands for Christian Inmates Association," he replied. "We meet every Thursday. It's like Bible study, only without the study. We talk, and pray, and we help each other cope. Come on out tomorrow and give it a try."

I was intrigued, and my nights were *always* free, so I figured I had nothing to lose.

When I walked onto the scene the next night, it was like coming home; people stood around engrossed in deep conversations as if they actually cared about each other, snacks lined the table, and a joyful laughter filled the room. About 20 of us were inmates; there was also a correctional officer and some civilian Christians who lived in the local area. I learned later that they came to Clinton each week as part of a new inmate ministry inspired by Chuck Colson, a former member of President Nixon's staff who had recently served prison time himself for his role in the Watergate scandal.

A man walked up and shook my hand with a firm grip. The delight in his face was unmistakable.

"Welcome," he said. "I'm Juan, CIA president. Don't ask me what I'm in here for, ask me what happened to me a year after I got here, 10 years ago."

"OK," I said, "what happened 10 years ago?"

"I became a new person in Christ."

We hit it off immediately. After a few minutes I felt as if I'd known him all my life. He taught the lesson that night, using personal stories from his past. Although he never stated what he had done, it had to be very serious to have been stuck here 10 years. His talk focused on what Jesus did and was doing for him and could do for anyone. He emphasized the word, "Anyone."

He inspired me. If Juan could go 10 years and still be that excited about what the Lord was doing in his life, I could make it too, as long as I had to.

As much as I enjoyed church services and Bible studies, those CIA meetings were the most memorable and inspiring evenings I experienced while at Clinton. We'd sing hymns, drink good coffee, and listen to different guest speakers that the civilians brought with them, and then inmates were encouraged to tell their stories, what they called "testimonies." During one of my first meetings Juan asked me to give mine and I did, to a point. I did not tell them of my former occupation but I did tell them about accepting Jesus on the lane, and how it changed my life. It was a beautiful time of fellowship.

Clinton has a renowned historical chapel behind The Wall that was hand-built by inmates in the '40s and named for Saint Dismas, the Good Thief, the man Jesus pardoned on the cross. However, we stayed on our side of The Wall, in our own, smaller chapel on the Annex grounds. I attended service every Sunday after seeing to the cows. About 20 or so other inmates also attended the services. Some came because they believed and others for the chance to get away. Some you couldn't tell. The important thing was, they were hearing about the Lord. I saw my former self in some of them. I'd stare at them and think, *that's the Joe from before, the guy who used to just sit there, not really hearing.*

Our preacher was an inmate who belonged to the Christian & Missionary Alliance, the same Protestant denomination as my church back home. I never asked him how he landed in our little country club, but stories were floating around that he'd had a serious problem with his wife. I told him where I was from and mentioned my pastor, Robert Burton, and he said, "Sure, I know Bob!" My pastor said later he'd never heard of him.

Regardless of his background, he preached a wonderful sermon every week. I felt almost as if I were back in Lockport. On my first Sunday, after we sang all three verses of "How Great Thou Art," the lyrics hit me so hard tears just poured down my face. I couldn't believe how much I'd changed since those days back in Audrey's church when I used to hide my annoyance behind a hymnal.

Most surprising to me was learning I had a decent singing voice. After all those years of just mouthing the words during Sunday services, I now found I couldn't be silent. And the lyrics! It was as if I were reading the words for the first time. They actually *meant* something to me. I sang with wild abandon, and the notes and harmonies just flowed.

The joy I received in that little chapel followed me back to the farm. I could always find something to be glad about. Other inmates apparently decided I was the real deal, because they continued to come to me to talk about my faith. At night they'd knock at my door, one after the other, as if each one had been waiting in the wings for the man before him to leave. I couldn't invite them in, so we'd sit in the doorway and I'd answer their questions as best I could. I had received a small stack of Bibles from my church that I gave away to anyone who asked for one. I even had some that were written in Spanish and Italian, which came in handy.

Occasionally, I thought I'd see lights start to flicker behind those blank stares as I talked to fellow inmates. However, there was so much shuffling of personnel, many inmates transferred out just as I thought they were on the cusp of understanding, and I'd never hear from them again. Eventually I realized that it didn't matter whether or not they accepted the Lord after talking with me. I was like Johnny Appleseed: there to plant, and to water a bit if time allowed.

The evening visitor traffic became so steady that I started getting up at 4 a.m. so I could keep writing to Audrey. Letters from home were keeping me grounded. They provided regular updates on Joey's progress at school (which was going quite well) and Jenny's battle with cancer (which was not), and the latest news from our congregation.

As it turned out, *I* was the latest news from our congregation. One of our parishioners, Richard Conley, formed a support group called Friends for Joe to ensure Audrey and I had everything we needed. The group prayed for us continually. They also set up a bank account in Audrey's name and started a fund-raising campaign to cover supplies and postage for the twice-monthly packages and to help off-set the cost of gas and hotels so she could visit me in the spring. People chipped in where they could, donating to newspaper drives and garage sales, and holding bake sales, spaghetti dinners, and car washes. The outpouring of support was so great, they raised enough money for Audrey to buy an airline ticket to fly up for a visit, and even rent a car while she was here. This meant she needn't wait for the snow to melt. She started planning a trip for just after Christmas. I could hardly wait!

When I first I read about FFJ in Audrey's letter, I cried. Yes, tears were becoming more and more common in this tough guy's life. I couldn't believe how good people were. I worried a bit that it might cause a problem among the church members because I wasn't sure everyone there thought I needed supporting, but I soon realized there'd been no need to worry. Judging from the number of cards and letters I received from the congregation—people I knew and total strangers, all offering support and prayers—I believe the project actually unified our congregation even more than it had been. Later, Audrey sent me a newspaper clipping about the FFJ project, quoting Pastor Bob saying, "We've never stopped believing in Joe, and now, through Friends for Joe, we can do something to help him and his family."

I felt as if God was reminding me daily that He hadn't forgotten me. At one point, I thought He'd carried things a bit too far. An inmate from our church in Lockport named Billy was serving his sentence at Attica when he heard about FFJ through some visiting parishioners, and Billy wanted to pitch in as well. He offered to take up a collection among the Christian inmates at Attica. Since the most any inmate could make was $1.35 a week, there was no way my conscience would allow me to accept their money, but I was certainly touched.

As Christmas drew near, various religious organizations near the prison did what they could to take the inmates' minds off their situation, or at least ease some of their loneliness. The Salvation Army did the best job of lifting our spirits, but not in the way they'd intended. It was about a week before Christmas when we saw them at the head of our chow line handing each inmate a package. The packages were all the same, and contained a copy of their magazine, *The War Cry*, as well as a banana, an orange, and assorted nuts still in their shells. They didn't provide nutcrackers, however, which are not the sort of thing stored in prison supply cabinets.

Back in the Annex we had piles of filberts, Brazilian almonds, walnuts, and pecans, but no way to crack them. This sparked an interesting game of improvisation; we smacked them with shoes, crushed them between rocks and under furniture, and chiseled away on them with anything we could find, but it just wasn't worth the work. Our makeshift tools had either no effect or they were so effective they left only pulverized shell piles. In the end, we just sat around and looked at them.

I have never spent a Christmas feeling as close to the Lord as I did that Christmas of 1977. As I wrote in a letter to Audrey, I had always considered myself a descendant of Scrooge, and I usually found Christmas to be a depressing time of the year, but at Clinton all of that changed.

I spent Christmas Eve cheering up inmates; some were miserable being so far from home on this day. They couldn't understand how I could be so joyous. I told them it wasn't me, but the Lord who made me whistle, sing, and hum. I couldn't change my situation, but I could certainly control how I reacted to it. Many of them confided that they wished they could be happy but it just wasn't possible. This gave me the opportunity to tell them about Jesus, and show them that they had lots to be happy about. A group of us gathered in the TV room, where I answered their questions about Jesus and let them know that God would never give up on them, no matter what they'd done. As we finished our talk, a television program came on called, *In Search of Noah's Ark*. We all stopped and watched; it was icing on the cake. Afterwards, we all pitched in some goodies and had a little Christmas party before going to bed.

While I lay in bed that night reading my Bible, the CO knocked on my door, entered my room, and handed me a package of cigarettes. It was wrapped with a Christmas bow and a little tag with an angel on it that said "Merry Christmas from Art."

Even though I didn't smoke, I was so thankful for his beautiful gesture. He said, "Merry Christmas, Tutt," and then went on his way to the next room, and to the other twenty or so. I know he purchased the cigs with his own money because nobody else we knew of received them. Even all these years later, as I consider the giver and the circumstances, I believe it's the nicest Christmas gift I've ever received.

In the morning, we went to the church and sang Christmas carols, and then the event organizers at the service split us into three groups to discuss the following questions:

- What is the true meaning of Christmas?
- What gift would you most like to receive this Christmas?
- If you could give a loved one any gift this Christmas, what would it be?
- What do you think the world would be like if Christ had never been born?

I was thoroughly impressed. The questions were so thought-provoking they stayed with me long after the service ended. I knew for certain what gift I wanted to give to a loved one. I thought of Joey, who after years of attending services with Audrey and me still hadn't accepted Christ; nor had my daughter, Linda. If I could give them anything that year it would be a clear understanding of the Truth. I knew, even as I prayed, that it would happen one day. I just needed to be patient.

I really missed my family that Christmas. Inmates were allowed only three phone calls home every month, and those were scheduled the month prior. My last December call was on the 22nd, and I'd savored every second, closing my eyes to imagine the house decorations, the smell of cinnamon and yeast wafting in from the kitchen, a toasty blaze in the fireplace...I had to quit before I started to tear up. I talked with Audrey, of course, and Joey, and then Mother and Dad. It was the best gift they could have given me.

Back on the dairy farm, Mr. Kovitch kept promoting me in my duties, to the point where, by January I'd become one of the milkers, responsible for my own string of 25 lady Holsteins. Milking was much more interesting and challenging than I'd expected. Running the milking machine required finesse, and timing, and the ability to know when to stop. If you milk her too long or not enough, a cow can get mastitis (a sore swelling of the teats). If that happened, we had to inject the cow with penicillin and then mark her because we couldn't use her milk until she was cleared. Well, I'm not too sure what I did differently, but I managed to get it right from the start. A mastitis case would pop up now and then on the other strings, and often for the milker across from me, but rarely for me. When the others remarked on my efficiency, I told them that was nothing. With the Lord, I could move mountains.

"Ah, we do that every day," they'd say. "Mountains of cow manure. C'mon, Holy Man, help us move these mountains!"

I still sensed wariness from Mr. Kovitch. Over time I developed a respect for him and his values. He was a tough man who demanded total obedience to rules and regulations, but he was also fair. One day there was a cutting tool missing from the storage area and Mr. Williams was questioning him about it. Few people were authorized to touch these tools because they could be turned into weapons, and I knew Mr. Kovitch would be in trouble if he couldn't produce it. I had just seen the cutters but I couldn't just say so, or Mr. Kovitch would look as if he didn't know what was going on. So I wrote a note: "I think the cutters are hanging on a peg in the shed above the heifer farm." I apologized for interrupting and said, "Sir, I'm sorry, did you see this note?

After the manager left, Mr. Kovitch came to me and said, "I'm glad you did that, because someone told me you were his informant."

I said, "Why would I be that? I wouldn't even be *your* informant."

As it turned out, someone had told him I was the manager's rat in an attempt to get him to give me the rotten jobs and treat me poorly. I had to say I respected him all the more for treating me so fairly regardless of his suspicions.

Over the next year, Mr. Kovitch and I became the closest thing to friends that an inmate and a guard could be. We never lost sight of the dividing line between us, but we grew to appreciate each other's company immensely.

One day he told me that he was running a side business after work, but that it was not doing well because people owed him a lot of money and just wouldn't pay. With my law background, I'd seen this happen to many people. I suggested that he write letters to those who owed him saying that, not he, but a parent company was about to put legal action on them. I also suggested he send the letters via registered mail, because people would pay attention to that. He did, and most of his clients paid what they owed.

As my responsibilities on the farm increased, I based my work philosophy on Paul's advice in his letter to the Colossians, which says, "*Whatsoever you do, do it heartily, as unto the Lord, and not unto men.*" I saw the worth of his words in the way inmates pulled together after I showed them God's way of working.

Each inmate on the farm was assigned one task, after which he stopped working until it came time to perform the chore again. One afternoon, after I'd finished my work, I saw an inmate pushing a heavy cart of hay up a hill and ran over to help him. His job was to feed the cows, so I stuck around to help. Then I helped another inmate wash the cows, which was no longer my job but I remembered how tedious it was and knew he'd appreciate the help.

Jacko came over to me and said, "Hey, Holy Man, you got somethin' to prove? Don't work so hard, man."

"I'm working for the Lord, Jacko," I said. "He wouldn't want me standing idle while someone else was working."

Jacko walked away shaking his head. A few other inmates stood around and snickered.

The next day, as the cart started up the hill I ran down to meet it. Darned if Jacko didn't beat me there, and the three of us got that thing up to the barn in no time at all. The grin on Jacko's face was priceless.

Other inmates started pitching in as well, and within a week or two we had formed a team—all for one. The work became much easier and we started to enjoy each other's company. I overheard an inmate say, "I don't know what this guy's got, but it sure is catchy."

By mid-January most of the inmates had accepted me, but not Stumpy, so named because he looked like a tree stump: as wide as he was tall. Stumpy was in for armed robbery after shooting up a bank. He was a mean, imposing man. He hated me, quite possibly because I was making friends on the farm. Whenever I walked by him, which was any time I went to the shower, he'd make a whirring noise and murmur snidely, "Calling all cars, calling all cars."

Stumpy never confronted me. He knew that if we fought, he'd be back behind The Wall before the second punch landed. However, this didn't stop him from sparring, inmate style, by bringing the CO into the conversation.

"So, Mr. Palmer," he said to the guard in front of me one evening, "What if I were to go to Tutt's room in the middle of the night and bang him over the head with a pipe? What would happen to me?"

After all God had done for me to that point, I'm ashamed to say I still let the Macho man in me have his way. I said to the CO, "Wait, Mr. Palmer. Before you answer that, what if Stumpy came in my room with a pipe and I broke both his arms and legs with it, what would happen to me?"

I was immediately sorry. No, I said to myself, that's the old Joe. I walked away quickly, praying for Stumpy, and asking forgiveness for myself. Nobody ever said being a Christian was easy, but I hadn't expected to fail quite so often.

That weekend, Audrey visited again, this time with Joey, who was on break from the university. A church friend of ours with a small plane flew them to nearby Utica so she could save her *Friends for Joe* money. She brought all kinds of canned tuna, crackers, soups, and some of her mother's canned beef, and of course, more pepperoni. I was particularly pleased to see my winter coat and a pair of gloves. The coat went right over my prison jacket. The gloves disappeared from my locker one day when I was at work. I had marked them with my name, so I'd recognize them if I saw them again. However, since they disappeared during the day, it wasn't likely an inmate took them. That's all I'm going to say about it except that, lest you make the wrong assumption, I believe that all but one of the Annex guards were highly respectful and quite professional; some even went out of their way to be kinder to us than they needed to be.

Another wonderful gift they brought that day was a fresh, hot pizza from a shop down the street. Pizza is like gold in prison. We ate it slowly in the visitors' room. I savored every bite almost as much as I savored the minutes with Audrey and Joey. She was managing at home, but I could see she was tired. I thanked God for all our church friends and family members who were back there taking care of her.

When the time came for them to leave, I kissed them both goodbye and took what was left of the pizza through the common area to my room, passing Stumpy in the television room. I returned and sat across from him, even though I had no interest in watching TV. Part of me wanted to say I wasn't afraid, and part of me wanted to make amends for my earlier taunt.

"Man, that stuff smelled good," he mumbled.

It was a small window of opportunity. "Stumpy," I said, "Would you like a piece of pizza?"

He looked at me with suspicion. But I said, "Of course you do. Hey, I'll get you some."

I walked to my room and came back with two pieces. When I held one out to him, he looked incredulous. "You'd give this to me?"

"Sure."

He eyed the piece I held out and said, "No, gimme the other piece."

I could tell he was still troubled, so I bit the ends off each one to show they were safe and offered them both, saying, "Here, which one do you want?"

As a grin crept across his face, I remembered a verse in Romans 12 that says not to take revenge out on your enemies but instead, "*If your enemy is hungry, feed him; if he is thirsty, give him something to drink; for by so doing you will heap burning coals on his head.*" I now understood what that meant. Stumpy just couldn't figure out why I would give him my pizza. By his logic, I should have sat there and eaten it in front of him, but this gift of kindness was much more effective. Stumpy and I never became close friends, but that night solidified our truce.

Now that I was "in" with the leaders, I continued to participate in the nightly gatherings. We talked about everything, sitting around the long table and sharing the canned food buffet. One Saturday night, after quite a few of our wives had visited, we made an Italian feast out of the fresh vegetables we'd received in our "care packages." It was somewhat comical, all of us in the common area slicing celery, tomatoes, cucumbers, onions and garlic with razor blades. But the salad was out-of-this-world delicious. Or, as my buddy Mario would say, "*Exsquisita!*"

As the evening wound down, Jacko started talking about someone in one of the other gangs who had crossed him that day and vowed, "I'm gonna take care of his ass."

I said, "That's not what the Bible says."

"Yeah, well what does the Bible say, Holy Man?"

"It says return good for evil."

"What does that mean?"

"If someone slaps you, you turn the other cheek. Do something nice. It will blow his mind."

"That's a lot of bull!"

"Well, look at me. Do you see me in trouble with anybody?"

"No."

"Don't you think people kind of like me, and respect me?"

"Yeah, but you're different."

Across the room, Stumpy was deep in thought. I wondered if he was thinking about the pizza. Big John, too, was quiet. Seeds were being planted.

A few nights later, Big John came and stood at my door in great distress. He seemed to be only a shell of his ferocious self, and on the point of losing control. He stammered quite a bit trying to start the conversation.

"Everything okay Big John?" I met him in the doorframe and touched his shoulder.

"No, Tutt, my sister is…she's got pneumonia. She's dying, man. You've got to pray for her."

It was heart wrenching to see this big man in such despair. I said, "I'm so sorry to hear that. Tell you what, kneel down and we'll pray together right now."

And he did. Right there in front of everyone. I was never so humbled about what God could do in a man as I was to see this oak-sized pillar of strength on his knees in the prison corridor, tears streaming down his face as he prayed for his sister's life. We prayed together for about 15 minutes, until his sobbing ebbed.

When he got up to leave, I saw an odd mix of awe and hope in his eyes.

"Keep praying John. I will too, right up until I fall asleep." Again I put a hand on his shoulder. "But whatever happens, remember that something wonderful happened here tonight."

He nodded and walked off in a daze.

The next day, a completely different Big John came to my door, a man almost bouncing with elation.

"He did it, Tutt! I just called home and she's not going to die! He heard us praying!"

That in itself was fantastic news, but I was even more thrilled by what he said next. He gave me a giant bear hug, and when he stood back, he said, "Tutt, I want to know everything there is to know about your God!"

The change in Big John after that was almost as dramatic as my own had been. He still had to maintain his gang head position, but he changed the way he talked to me and to others. Although he didn't yet accept Jesus as his Savior, he started coming to Bible study, and when he came, his people had to come.

He'd walk into the common area and announce in his booming voice, "I'm going to study the Word of God. WOULD ALL OF YOU LIKE TO GO?"

He could be quite influential.

Each day I'd marvel anew about God's constant provision. I don't know how to explain it, except that I felt so unworthy of all that was going on with me that it heightened my appreciation for every good thing. The more I studied the Bible, the more I realized that the Holy Spirit was showing me how to find God in nearly every situation. I'd wake up excited about what the Lord might accomplish that day. I started seeing my fellow inmates as either hungry, or disguising their hunger. The same person who, in a group, would announce with disdain, "I don't want to hear any of that religious stuff" would appear in my doorway that night with a hundred questions.

We all celebrated when Juan, the CIA president, was granted his parole. I hated to see him go. I'd learned a lot from him and we'd become quite close. Juan asked me to take the CIA helm. I was thrilled to do so. Those meetings meant a lot to me, and I considered it an honor to lead the group.

Somehow, I also acquired an unofficial role as the Annex's inmate mediator. More than once I'd hear a heated argument culminate with, "Oh yeah? Well, let's ask Holy Man. He won't lie."

Occasionally, the arguments turned into fist fights. One day it was Jacko, who had taken on a man twice his size over some comment made in the TV room. Fortunately, I arrived just as the big man was winding up a blow that would have sent Jacko to the infirmary. I ran right between them and shouted, "Hey! What's the matter with you two? Do you like it here? Is this worth going back to Population? Think, Jacko. Think!"

Jacko whimpered. "Well he said –"

"It doesn't matter what he said. All that matters is if you like it here, you gotta stop."

I glared at both of them until they simmered down and mumbled, "Yeah, I guess you're right."

I made them shake hands, which they did, growling at each other, but 20 minutes later they were watching a fight on TV, acting as if it had never happened.

One other time I raced foolishly toward a commotion that could have turned into a very painful experience. A crowd had gathered, but they let me through, and as I stepped into the center, I found myself face-to-face with Kuba, the man I'd arrested for dealing about five years earlier. We'd more or less kept a respectful distance from each other since I'd arrived, but on this day, he was in the middle of exchanging blows with another very large man; both of them were weight lifters. It was like Fight Night on WWF. I ducked down under a punch and stepped between them. To this day I don't know what made me do it. If either of them had swung and missed, I would have been knocked into oblivion. Kuba might have even thrown in a blow to my face on purpose, and nobody would have suspected a thing. But there I stood, arms out like a referee, yelling, "Think! Think!" All of a sudden, they just stopped.

Apparently, neither wanted to be known as the one who hit the Holy Man.

Who do they think I am, exactly?

Kuba stared at me with a quiet intensity that was almost unnerving, but I had to push forward. I said the same things to them I'd said to Jacko: "Remember life behind The Wall and ask yourselves if you really want to go back there." Their anger fizzled, and men apologized to each other and shook hands. Just like that, the crisis ended. Never could I have imagined, back in that courtroom listening to my sentence, that one day I would step into such a lion's den and emerge unscathed.

I received a letter from Joey that January that brought tears to my eyes. He said he was getting great grades in school and was considering accepting Christ. Turns out he had watched a movie called *The Late, Great Planet Earth* with his friends and wound up telling *them* about Christ. They talked into the early hours, with Joey showing them events in his Bible and telling them how it had been growing up in a spirit-filled church. He said he suddenly realized the significance of the teachings he'd received in our church back in Lockport and decided he would start attending Campus Crusade events and Bible studies at school. All anyone can say to news like that is Praise the Lord!

Toward the end of January, I developed a limp. Mr. Kovitch noticed and called me over.

"What's going on there?" He pointed at my foot.

"It's these shoes, I think." I pulled one off and rubbed my foot. "They're quite narrow, and I've developed a spur."

"Go sign up for an appointment. Get that taken care of before it gets worse."

"I did, Sir." I put the shoe back on. "About a week ago. They haven't called me in yet. I also put in a request for shoes that fit, but that's gone nowhere either."

I thought Mr. Kovitch was going to explode.

"If you don't hear from the infirmary tomorrow, I'm putting you on sick call!" He seethed. "What do they think you guys are? For Pete's sake, the *vet* comes quickly enough when there's a sick cow!"

Two days later, they called me in, but instead of actually treating the injury, the doc prescribed pain meds and bed rest. The entire ordeal was a preview of sorts to what I would face the next month after my Great Fall.

Audrey came to my rescue by mailing me my work boots. They hugged my feet like an old friend and my wound healed quickly after that.

Although I'd become acclimatized, the relentless Dannemora winter was wearing me down. I'd never seen anything like it. We had 72 inches of snow in January alone—the stuff was practically waist-high all month, and temperatures got down as low as -12 degrees. But it was the wind that got to me, gale-force blusters coming up from the valley that would sting our eyes and push us down, and make us fight for every step. Those cows didn't know how good they had it, staying indoors all winter.

One thing I noticed, no matter how hard the winter storms raged, I cannot think of a single time the local civilians failed to show up for a CIA meeting. It was as if they knew how much we counted on them. What amazing dedication they had.

As February approached, I added farm maintenance to my job descriptions. I seemed to have a knack for fixing things. Nobody was more surprised to learn this than Ol' Joe Tutt. I repaired the auger in the silo; repaired milking machines, and, when ten men tried and failed to raise a sick cow, I devised a sling with some rope that lifted her using only two men. It got to the point where the CO's first response to a problem would be to yell, "Where's Tutt?"

When I told Audrey about my increasing responsibilities, she said I was getting to be like Joseph in the Bible, who was sent to Egypt as a slave, thrown into prison, and then rose in stature until he was the pharaoh's right-hand man. I felt a fleeting concern that I might start thinking more of myself than I should. I prayed the Lord would ensure I stayed humble. With hindsight, I think I probably shouldn't have prayed that, because a few days later, he arranged to bring me to the ground. Literally.

But that story is for the next chapter.

The Rusty Shovel

Spring-Summer, 1978

Before I tell you about my fall, I must clear up a misconception I see developing on these pages. What you're reading are glimpses of a wider picture that was not always pretty.

Granted, the Lord arranged for something that could have been a dark, depressing experience for me to be instead a time of light and joy; however, I did not *enjoy* being in prison. I missed my family. I wanted desperately to be with Jenny, whose cancer was worsening. I endured blistering cold, and fought through snow drifts and blizzard conditions to get in and out of the barns, morning and night. I did not like being told what I could and couldn't do, and where I could and couldn't go. I wrestled often with bouts of depression and self-pity, and I had days where I didn't want to get out of bed to tend to the farm.

The only difference between my situation and that of many others in that prison was that I had Jesus. The old Joe, that self-sufficient, egotistical cop who felt sorry for the church goers, he wouldn't have made it through. I'm sure of that. The only reason I was able to climb out of the valleys was because I relied on the Lord, my Bible, prayer, and fellowship with other Christians. During my deepest times of depression, I focused on Paul, who was a prisoner himself when he penned the words in his letter to the Philippians, "...for I have learned, in whatever state I am, therewith to be content," and who, despite suffering greatly from an affliction that God would not remove, praised the Lord zealously for His sufficient grace.

Like Paul, I considered myself an unworthy wretch, which made the Lord's love toward me all the more amazing. I started each day in prayer, and nearly every day I found my way to that place of awe and gratitude, a place of remembering that my story was not about me; it was God's story, about what He could do in an arrogant man's life.

That said, our story resumes on a crisp February morning, just as the harsh weather had begun to ebb. Mr. Kovitch had said we were experiencing a rather mild winter, which surprised me because I couldn't imagine anything worse. It was still cold, but dry and sunny.

I and a team of inmates were storing a few hundred bales of hay in the barn. I braced myself atop a 15-foot ladder by leaning against the barn's loft window so I could catch bales from Jacko, who stood below me in the bed of a high farm truck. As I grabbed each bale I turned and tossed it into the loft, where two other inmates stacked them. I enjoyed the work, with its catchy rhythm of grunts, swishing hay, and a steady thump-thump of the ladder as it slid back and forth over loose straw at the loft entrance. A real farmer would have pegged some nails on either side of the ladder to keep it still, but this city boy was more interested in maintaining the rhythm and finishing the job quickly.

Naturally, the ladder slipped off the sill and sent me flying. Jacko later told me I did a flip in the air and then landed on my back across the ladder, which had made it to the ground first.

The fall knocked the wind out of me and sent excruciating pain through every cell of my body. I lay still, trying to refill my lungs and assess my injuries. The pain was particularly sharp around my heart, making me wonder briefly if this was how my life would end. Forcing myself to be calm, I began to pray, *Jesus heal me*, and with a loud, sucking wheeze I drew in an enormous gasp of air. Inmates scrambled around me asking questions and yelling for help, and I heard Mr. Kovitch hollering in the background, but their noises were in another world far away.

Still praying, *Jesus heal me*, I focused on my toes and fingers, willing them to move, and they did. I lifted a hand to my ribs and felt around gingerly; I was pretty sure they weren't broken but man, did they hurt. Then the pain in my heart began to ease, and I regained the frequency of the voices around me.

After what seemed like ages, but what turned out to be only a minute or so, I looked up and saw Jacko over me, hand stretched out. I grabbed the hand and he pulled me carefully to my feet.

I had a sore knee, bruised ribs, and sharp pains in my left arm and shoulder. I'm certain it would have been worse had it been a warmer day. I believe my Farmer Joe issue—long underwear, coveralls, sweater, and parka—padded my fall.

A guard drove me to the infirmary. The only staff member on duty (to this day I don't believe he could possibly have been a doctor) was busy chatting with a visiting nurse and seemed bothered by my intrusion. He took one look at me and said, "Wiggle your fingers."

All ten moved on command.

"You're fine," he said, and sent me back to work.

Incredulous, I tried to explain my injuries, but he told me to leave. I couldn't even get pain medicine, for Pete's sake. I complained to my CO, but all he said was, "You have been examined by the doc. There is nothing I can do for you."

My shoulder and arm throbbed, so I fashioned my own sling by tying a belt around my neck and under my forearm. This eased some of the pain, but I was certain something was broken. Despite all my attempts to get it looked at, the standard response was that without x-rays to prove a problem existed there could be no treatment, which seemed somewhat backward to me. The pain was so acute, it took all I had just to tie my shoes each day. Mr. Kovitch tried to intervene, but the manager told him to just give me lighter work.

When Audrey visited, eight days after my fall, she was horrified at my belt-sling. Boy, did she make noise around that place! I don't know what she said or to whom, but all of a sudden I was the center of attention. People were going out of their way to be nice to me, and they kept shoving paperwork under my nose. Sadly, I believe they were just trying to cover themselves. Even so, it was another day and a half before my arm was x-rayed.

Surprise, surprise, I had a fracture.

The prison physician sent me to an orthopedic doctor in nearby Plattsburg who had a good reputation in the region. I liked him; he treated me like a person. He x-rayed my arm, left shoulder, and left knee and had me wait in the cast room, anticipating, I guess, that he would be putting a cast on my arm.

He joined me with the x-rays and stared at them for quite a while.

"How long ago did this happen?"

"Eleven days ago," I answered.

He shook his head and sighed, "There's no point in a cast now."

The doc wrapped my arm with an ace bandage and gave me a real sling. He told me to exercise the arm as much as I could stand and to come back in three weeks. My shoulder and knee had only been badly banged up and had nearly healed.

When I returned to my room in the Annex, I found the doctor's assistant had sent up some pain pills.

Unbelievable. Might have been nice to have 11 days ago.

My prison counselor was livid when I told him what had happened. He suggested I get my lawyer to write to the superintendent and to Albany, and to bring a law suit against the state. He said he'd seen many similar cases of poor medical treatment here, and that perhaps someone with my background could do something to correct it. I pondered and prayed about this for quite some time, and decided it was the right thing to do. I hesitated to start anything, but what had happened to me was quite unacceptable. To make matters worse, about five days later I was summoned for another set of x-rays. When I explained that the physician in Plattsburgh had taken care of it and reminded them of the dangers posed by too much radiation exposure (I was married to an RN, don't forget), they tried to get me to sign a statement for "refusal of medical treatment."

The worst part of the ordeal, other than the pain, was that I couldn't work on the farm. I spent almost two months recuperating in the Annex, nearly going crazy with boredom. I read every book I could lay my hands on, particularly personal testimonies, and I wrote many letters. I also befriended people who were in the Annex during the day, like the porter (an inmate who cleaned the common areas), and the guards on the day-shift. Most of them had not met Jesus, so I made sure to introduce them. The porter eventually started attending our CIA meetings, and then Sunday services.

Mr. Kovitch visited me while I was on sick leave, and so did Ben Vaughn, the senior civilian worker on the farm. They both said the farm was going to pot without me. Mr. Kovitch kept checking in to see when I could go back to work, but I know he was more worried about me than the farm. The way he fussed, you'd think we were related.

Big John also came to my room one night and asked me to teach him how to use the Bible and what to read. I saw the leader in him, and a thirst for knowledge. Since his sister's bout with pneumonia we'd talked often about the Lord, but this was the first time he tried to learn on his own. A thought flashed through my mind that the Lord had chosen him to replace me as CIA president. I had to chuckle at that. First, I wasn't leaving any time soon, and he hadn't accepted Christ yet, so how could he lead others to do so? Still, stranger things have happened.

Then the flip-side of that musing occurred to me; I was already thinking of leaving. I'd only been here five months. I still didn't even know the "minimum" end of my sentence, which would be determined in an upcoming Minimum Period of Imprisonment (MPI) board. The least amount of time they could give me would be 18 months. Big John and I had our hearings scheduled for September 7, but Jacko's board was coming up in March.

I met with my lawyer in early March to get the ball rolling on the lawsuit. My brother Sam had written and put in his two cents. He wanted me to sue everyone, including the governor's janitor. I wasn't bitter about my treatment or looking for revenge, and if it had only been me I wouldn't have done anything, but as my story spread among the inmates and guards, people started bringing me their own horror stories. I decided that, in the name of humanity, something had to be done, and I had the opportunity. Regrettably, unless the state was forced to pay money, nothing would ever change, and so a civil suit was our only option. The state scheduled my hearing for July.

While I recuperated, I also befriended the cook in our mess hall, an Irish inmate called Red who had a fiery crimson crew cut and a temper to match. I helped him write a few letters to his wife, who was threatening to leave him. For weeks he had been looking forward to his upcoming MPI board, figuring that since he'd been at Clinton for 15 months, he might be near the end of his sentence. He thought he could keep her from leaving if only he could get home. Instead, the board set his minimum at 27 months, nine more than he'd expected.

As if that weren't enough, he also lost his job as our cook. Word of his domestic problems had reached the ears of the prison officials, and because they considered him a good candidate for escape they removed his outside clearance. Before he left our complex I tried to talk to him about Jesus, but he was too bitter to listen. I prayed for him and sent his name to my church family back in Lockport so they would pray as well. His situation made my problems seem so very small. I put extra kisses in my letter to Audrey that night.

Mr. Kovitch moved up to replace Mr. Williams as farm manager in mid-March, right about the same time the prison doctors agreed to let me return to work. My shoulder had improved a great deal, but it still wasn't right, and my arm seemed to have a permanent twist at the elbow. Mr. K put me in the most logical place: in the dairy office, to work as a clerk.

I received an odd reception. Throughout my recovery time, the guys had seen me every evening; we talked and joked and ate together as usual. But the moment I got to the farm, you'd have thought they hadn't seen me in the seven weeks. They gathered around me, each one eager to clap my back and give me the latest farm news.

On the other hand, the porter in the Annex missed our conversations; he actually urged me to complain that I couldn't work so I could stay there with him.

The clerk's job was fun. For a little while the sheer disorder made me feel like Felix Unger from the Odd Couple. I jumped right in, straightening files, setting up tracking systems, and incorporating some changes to improve administrative efficiency. Ben Vaughn was thrilled to see order around the place.

At the end of March, I was promoted again, this time to Inmate Farm Manager. Mr. Kovitch pretty much gave me free rein, and in exchange I made sure that farm ran like a clock. I essentially handled all the books (even tracking the guards' time sheets for Payroll) and ensured the cows had everything they needed, from feeding and milking supplies to medical treatment.

Medical issues are a big deal on a dairy farm. In addition to mastitis, which came from poor milking practices, two other common issues that required immediate attention were thrush, a bacterial parasite that lodged in the hooves after a cow stepped in manure, and water on the knee, which was a swelling that occurred when a heifer bumped her knee. I figured out a way to draw the fluid out using two needles, one to equalize the pressure, and the other to draw the fluid. Once we removed the fluid, the cows healed quickly.

I was also one of the few people allowed to handle knives; the farm kept two: a long narrow knife used to butcher pigs, and a skinning knife to skin them. We had to record each time we drew them and returned them; their whereabouts were closely monitored.

It occurred to me one day that I was using every skill I'd learned as a police officer and then some. I employed not only my clerical skills (all those man hours spent filing warrant applications and arrest documents didn't go to waste), but life skills as well. It was interesting how many aspects of farm management require quick or practical thinking; the rest required dedication and hard work.

During my undercover days, I'd developed a resourcefulness that proved invaluable on the farm. I could make or acquire just about anything. One day Jacko brought me some leather harnesses that were starting to rot, and I didn't think twice but asked Audrey to bring up some linseed oil on her next visit. It would have taken months to obtain linseed through the prison requisition system, but she brought it in my care package the following week. I tried to bring the box back to my room from the visitor's station, but the guard pulled out the oil because he didn't know what it was. I went to the office and told Mr. Kovitch what had happened and he stormed out. Five minutes later he came back with the oil.

My new responsibilities came with a raise. I was now earning 95 cents a day. In that night's letter to Audrey I wrote, "Oh, how I'm dreading income tax day—this will surely put me in a higher bracket!"

By June I could almost straighten my arm, yet the inmates and COs still treated me like an invalid. I couldn't pick up a single thing without someone rushing in to lift it for me, which made me uncomfortable. I told them I was supposed to exercise it, but they'd respond, "Exercise in your room."

Even Mr. Kovitch was mothering. He'd tell other COs to give up their chairs to me if there wasn't one available in the office. And they'd apologize when they realized I had nowhere to sit. Unbelievable!

When Jacko left to go before the MPI board, we all rooted for him and prayed. He had a 0-5 year sentence for hitting his friend over the head with a pipe, fracturing the man's skull. To make matters worse, he then took his friend's money and stole his car. However, by the time of his board, after serving 10 months, Jacko was a completely different person than he'd been at the time of his crime—one who could control his temper and worked hard at his tasks. He came back from the board dejected and in shock. They'd set his minimum to 38 months.

That night, Jacko came to my doorway and we talked for hours. I convinced him that regardless of how bleak things appeared he could change things with the right attitude. He could become angry and vengeful, which would lead to misery and more likely additional time behind bars, or he could rely on the Lord and try to make something useful of his remaining time here. He left deep in thought, not at all like the Jacko I'd met six months earlier.

A few days later, Red, our former cook, sent me a request through the grapevine to meet him at the barber shop, which is the only place we could talk because he was housed in another building. He was being transferred. He all but cried, saying good-bye.

After he left I found myself musing about how many people I'd crossed paths with at Clinton. We'd link up for a short time and then part, sometimes forever. I'd pray, knowing in my heart the Lord would continue working with them through other believers along their own paths until they could fully recognize the truth. Still I wondered, did Johnny Appleseed ever get to see any of his trees fully grown?

I visited the ortho doc in Plattsburgh three times. I still couldn't straighten my arm without something in there shifting in an unusual manner, but there was nothing he could do about it.

"You'll have to learn to live with it," he said. "You'll probably have it the rest of your life."

I decided to just accept it, as if I had any choice. It didn't limit my activities. In fact, as soon as I returned to the farm that day, I helped slaughter 10 pigs. Aside from all the noise, it was a welcome change to have bacon and sausage in the mess hall for a few days.

We began to hear rumors that the Attorney General's Office had investigated Clinton's medical treatment procedures and didn't like what they found. The lead physician was relieved of duty, and inmates who went to sick call returned saying the general attitude and treatment in the clinic seemed greatly improved. I did not withdraw my suit.

Nappy, the cook who replaced Red, turned out to be a disaster. He could only cook pancakes for breakfast, and for most other meals he usually served cold cuts. I asked Mr. Kovitch if he'd let me cook a meal. He said, "Whaddya mean, cook? Like, you can fry eggs?"

"No," I said, "I can cook anything."

He told me to go for it.

That first night, I made chicken cacciatore and graham cracker pit-pudding with cherries, using a recipe I learned from Ma. I'd also seen a cardoon patch out back so I asked Nappy and his helper to pick and clean them. Cardoon is an artichoke-like plant that's popular in Sicily. I breaded them with cracker crumbs (we were out of bread crumbs) and baked them. You should have heard the "yucks" and "ughs" everyone made before they tasted them, but I made believers out of just about everyone. Nappy was none too pleased, but hey, a man can only eat so many pancakes.

I took Nappy under my wing in the kitchen for a few weeks, teaching him basic cooking principles in between my farm duties. As we worked, Nappy kept asking me about Jesus, so I kept talking. After the first week, he attended church services with me and then went to Bible study. He told everyone it was just so he could get out of work early, but he'd also ask me to pray for his brother who was having all sorts of problems. Next thing I knew, I was overhearing him talking to *others* about Jesus. At times like that, all you can do is praise the Lord!

Nappy was reclining precariously on a straight-backed chair in the kitchen one day when he dozed off and fell backwards, hitting his head on the concrete wall. It knocked him silly for a while, and his pupils dilated. He insisted he was okay but I made another inmate take him to sick call. They immediately admitted him to the hospital for a traumatic brain injury. He came back on fire for the Lord, telling everyone how close he came to dying. After that, he sure wasn't going to church just to get out of work. God does indeed act in mysterious ways.

With Nappy on bed rest we were again without a cook. We had to have one, so I told Mr. Kovitch I could take the job. He asked me if I could manage both jobs until Nappy returned, but quickly retracted the idea.

"No, I need you too much on the farm to bury you in the kitchen," he said. "Pick someone and teach him to cook."

I laughed. "Just like that, teach someone to cook? Like it can be done in 20 minutes?"

When he realized what he'd said, he started laughing too.

"Joe," he said, "I think I'm losing my marbles."

He might not have caught the slip, but I did, and it meant a lot to me to know I was "Joe" to him.

So again the routine changed. In the mornings I'd run to the mess hall at the top of the hill to fix the coffee, then come back down in time to record the weight of the cows' milk. Then I'd go back up the hill to fix breakfast and start lunch, then back to the dairy for bookkeeping, then dinner, then the evening milking and weighing…it was exhilarating, but quite exhausting. After a few weeks we learned that Nappy wasn't coming back. It took another three months for Mr. Kovitch to find another cook. I can't say I was sorry when my replacement came, but it was fun while it lasted.

Nappy's replacement was Crazy Stella, who could cook well enough, but he was involved in a cult that was led by some Tibetan "prophet." I'd been reading about how false prophets pulled people away from the truth; Crazy Stella was the first man I knew to get caught up in such fantasy. He gave me two books to look over regarding this cult and asked for my opinion. I thumbed through them and felt sick; they were cleverly written and appealed to ego and self-gratification, which are the devil's greatest tools. I opened my Bible and went to him with some scripture that I hoped would shed light for him. I also left him a copy of the Four Spiritual Laws (a set of Biblical principles that explain the basics of Christianity...I'll enclose those at the end of this book), and I prayed for him. It was heartbreaking to see how easily people are led astray.

Back at the Annex, as if I weren't busy enough, I started teaching English to Mario and a few of my other Italian friends. Mario was a star pupil. We began with some translation exercises, in which I'd write some sentences in Italian for them to translate into English. Of course, I wrote about Jesus. As I'd hoped, the conversation occasionally derailed into a Biblical question and answer session. One night as soon as they arrived for class one of them said, "Can we forget Italian tonight and get into this Jesus thing?"

Other inmates continued to visit me in the evenings with questions about faith. Some would come once or twice, and others were regulars like Lorenzo, a young Hispanic man I met in the infirmary one weekend when I'd come down with a bug and got stuck on bed rest. I had just finished lunch and was reading my Bible when I noticed him pacing nearby. He'd get as far as my bed and turn around and walk back. He did this several times before deciding to go for it.

"Yo, man," he asked, "is that a Bible?"

"Yes it is." I held it up. "Have you read it?"

"Nah," he said. "I tried man, but all the 'thous' and 'thines' and 'begats' were too much for me. I just wish they would write one of these in English."

I had to hide my smile. "They do," I said. "It's called the Living Bible. If you want, I'll bring you one tomorrow."

His eyes lit up. "Really? I heard you gave them out, but I didn't believe it. Yes, I'd like that," he said. Then he stood at my bed, not quite ready to leave.

"Read me something from the Bible," he said, "Anything!"

I was reading Genesis at the time, so I picked up where I'd left off...

> *Then Joseph said to his brothers, "Come close to me." When they had done so, he said, "I am your brother Joseph, the one you sold into Egypt! And now, do not be distressed and do not be angry with yourselves for selling me here, because it was to save lives that God sent me ahead of you. For two years now there has been famine in the land, and for the next five years there will be no plowing and reaping. But God sent me ahead of you to preserve for you a remnant on earth and to save your lives by a great deliverance.*

"That's nice," Lorenzo said quietly. "My Mama, she says I need to read that book, so I'm glad to have one. If you give me one, I will read it."

"Your Mama's a smart woman," I said. I will get it to you tomorrow, and if you have any trouble with any of the words, bring it to me and I'll translate for you."

As Lorenzo left the room, I found myself re-reading the passage, as if for the first time. How masterfully orchestrated was Joseph's life. Despite everything he'd been through at the hands of others— kidnapped, sold as a slave, put into prison for a crime he didn't commit—Joseph continued to trust and praise the Lord. Then, when the story had run its full course, and he could finally see his life and his purpose from God's perspective, he saw a life of riches and blessings, and a purpose more wonderful than anything he could have imagined for himself. I thought of all the people God had sent my way since I arrived at Clinton, and all the seeds that were being planted, and I knew that how I got here didn't matter one bit. He was up to something big. I won't see the whole picture until I get to Heaven, but when I do, it's going to be magnificent!

Lorenzo became one of my nightly visitors. One night, we were talking about the book of John and he asked, "Hey, Holy Man, why didn't Jesus do anything to that Judas guy that squealed on Him? I'd a taken care of him for good! And another thing…why did Jesus patch up the crook's ear when Peter tried to do him in? That guy had it coming!"

I'd started to notice that this seemed to be a recurring point of issue among the inmates. As with Stumpy and Jacko, two of the hardest concepts for them to grasp seemed to be love and forgiveness. To them, the idea of not retaliating for a wrong was more foreign than any language barrier. I learned that once they truly understood the magnitude of God's forgiveness, it was a short leap to realizing that He could forgive them as well, but without that knowledge, they couldn't believe. I believe this was also keeping Big John from accepting Christ—he thought his crimes too big and too numerous to forgive.

Our little Sunday morning congregation at the chapel continued to grow, as did the list of volunteers who took turns helping with the service. I had joined the choir, and, like the others, read scriptures, helped with communion, and served wherever the pastor needed us. With regard to communion, we could not have wine or even grape juice with our bread. Apparently the yeast in the bread can combine with juice to ferment into booze (this had better potential than the smashed raisin theory, at least). So, we sipped water and said Jesus would turn it to wine as we drank it, the way He did in the Bible. I'm amazed by how seriously we took that.

One Sunday in early June, as I took my turn reading the scriptures before the sermon, I looked out over the pews of inmates and spotted a tall Black man, staring at me with a grin so wide it was nearly blinding. I knew that face! It was one I'd never expected to see again—Harl—the man who had flipped that first note into my cell at Attica!

I wrestled my way through the reading; part of me wanted to pay due reverence to the Lord while the other part tugged like a police dog on its leash. As soon as I finished, I made a beeline for his pew and we embraced heartily. I invited him to Bible class that night, where I was thrilled to finally be able to thank him for the note and learn his story.

Harl had been even further down in a pit than I was when he found Jesus. He'd been a pimp, a dope pusher, and a gambler, but he gave all that up the day he cried out to the Lord for help and God answered immediately. To tell his story would double the length of this book, so I'll just say that it was so inspiring, we asked him to give his testimony the following Sunday during service and he did. As he spoke of the forgiveness he'd received through repentance and establishing a relationship with the Lord, I watched Lorenzo listening intently, and I do believe I saw the light bulb come on over his head. I realized that God had brought Harl to our little chapel to connect with Lorenzo in a way that I could not.

A few nights later, Lorenzo came to my room in tears after learning that his 3-year-old son had died of pneumonia.

"I don't get it, Tutt." Lorenzo slid to the floor. "That boy meant everything to me. Why would God just take him just when I was thinking of becoming a Christian?"

"Lorenzo, we don't know that God *did* take him." I felt inadequate, wanting to say the right thing, but there were many things about God I still didn't understand. "This world is so full of sickness and evil, being Christian doesn't mean bad things won't happen. We can only be sure God knows *what* happened, and that He knows about your pain. He wants you to love Him anyway. That's pretty much what faith is all about."

Lorenzo sat for a long time, processing. Then he tilted his head back against the door frame and stared upward through his tears, as if trying to see heaven.

"Do you think my boy is with Him?"

"I'm sure of it."

We talked all evening, and we prayed together, asking God to watch over his boy. Lorenzo came to my door every chance he could find after that. He believed his son was in Heaven, and he wanted to be sure he'd be going there as well. Over time, he accepted that God could forgive him. I was so glad Harl had connected with him in time...as if it were coincidence.

In mid-June, I went to court about my injuries. The guards transferred me to Buffalo, and I spent about a week at the county jail where I'd been locked up that first night. I still knew most of the guards there, and many stopped in to say hello. I suspected it was because they'd heard rumors about how much Tough Ol' Joe Tutt had changed, and had to come see for themselves.

It was a quick hearing, and the court found the State negligent. I ended up making about $400 after attorney fees, but more importantly, this case changed the way inmates' injuries were treated in New York prisons.

When I returned to the Annex, I was somewhat overwhelmed by the welcoming reception I received. I marveled at the idea that I might be popular, and I wondered, how many inmates had God influenced through me? It was a moment of pride that brought immediate shame. I pondered the many times I'd written to Audrey or my church family about inmates who were taking an interest in God, and how He was opening their eyes through me. Was I boasting? Was it okay to feel pride about this? I didn't write to her for a few days, so I could work it out in my head.

Then one morning I was digging a hole for a post—not with the proper tools, but with a rickety, rusty shovel with a loose head that felt as if it would fly off at any moment. In fact, I used the handle end to round off the hole because it was more efficient. I finished the job though, and you wouldn't know by looking at the post how bad the shovel had been. That's when it hit me. I was that shovel. It was okay to take pride in the way God worked through me because the shovel wasn't the star. The shovel's only job was to be available, and to hold itself together long enough for the Digger to work a miracle. When the shovel boasts, it's about what the Digger accomplished. I resumed my letter writing, and in fact, since I realized that some of my letters home could be shovel handles in their own right, I continued to write boldly whenever the Lord put me in other people's lives to teach them something about Himself. I also examined the idea of being popular and determined that it's not about my popularity at all. People were drawn to me because I was happy and they wanted what I had. Happiness is just one more tool in the Digger's belt.

Lefty and Shorty were two of my favorite inmates. They weren't tough at all; in fact, they were two of the most easy-going people I've ever met. They were Puerto Rican inmates, both from New York City, who had committed a crime together. As the story goes, they were caught looting during a city-wide black-out. The severity of their sentence was based on volume, and they'd amassed so much loot it was classified as grand larceny. The two picked on each other constantly, but were the best of friends.

Lefty joined the milking crew. One day when he brought his milk to me for weighing, I decided to have a little fun with him.

"Hey, Lefty," I said. "When did we meet?"

"I dunno," he said.

"I'll bet that I was there when you were born."

"Get outta' here."

"What do you want to bet? How about a cig?"

"You're on."

"Well," I said, "not only was that eye there, but the other eye was as well."

He roared and reached for his cigarettes, but I waved them aside, chuckling.

After that, whenever I saw him, he'd put one hand over his eye and laugh.

Then Shorty came by to say, "I hear you got Lefty real good."

Like many others, Lefty and Shorty became interested in our nightly discussions about faith during their time at the Annex, but neither would admit it to the other. They were covert, as if afraid to admit to each other they were too weak to make it without Jesus. It was particularly comical the day Lefty came to my door and said, "I bet if I ask you for one of them Bibles, you're going to tell Shorty."

I handed it to him, saying, "Why would I do that?"

He shoved it under his shirt, thanked me, and snuck away.

What he didn't know was that a few days earlier, Shorty had come by and the same scene had played out. Shorty left with a Bible under his shirt as well.

In July, Mr. Kovitch wrote out my evaluation report and let me read it. On the blank line under the prompt, "Needs supervision/needs little supervision," he wrote, "Tutt supervises us."

I laughed and said, "You're not really going to submit that, are you?

He said, "You're damn right I am."

I chuckled, and praised the Lord for His goodness.

The highlight of every week was the CIA meeting. As president, my job was to open the meeting and lead the discussion. I made sure there was always a speaker, whether a visiting outsider, a church pastor, or even another inmate with a prepared lesson. I kicked off the meetings by welcoming new attendees. Then I'd open with prayer or ask for a volunteer to pray. I'm tickled to say many did. It was refreshing to see the Lord change so many people who'd never had the opportunity to hear the saving grace of Jesus, and it baffled my mind to think they had to come to prison to hear it.

Inmates came to the meetings for various reasons, and I'll admit, a lot were there for the break in routine, but they still heard the truth while they were there. Every Wednesday I'd invite any inmates still on the farm at closing time. I remember one night when I invited seven of my guys and four said they would attend. All four were among the farm's toughest characters. When they agreed to go, they took a bit of a ribbing from some of the others until a big muscle-man named Tank said, "HEY! If Tutt said it's nice, it's nice. You know he don't lie. Now if someone wants a punch in the mouth, keep talking!"

It may not have been what Paul had in mind when he said not to be ashamed of the Gospel, but it would do in a pinch.

The important thing is that the four were really impressed by the testimonies and joy they witnessed that night. Not only did they return the next week, but they brought the other three with them. Willingly, I hope. One of the newer members was Kuba, who rarely participated but stood alone against the wall and listened. He hadn't spoken to me since I broke up his fight, and I couldn't blame him. I was just glad to see him there so I never addressed him directly.

As July seared onward, we all thought we would melt from the heat and humidity, which tended to affect our moods on the farm. We did what we could to stay positive. I kept a small flower garden outside the office near a rock wall that made a great bench, where I sat when things were quiet. I spent many evening hours there.

We also used humor to lighten the strain. I was in the barn one morning, when Benny the chicken man stormed through, complaining about the heat. He was a new guy, and a city slicker to boot. I winked at one of the milkers and said, "You're right, Benny, it sure is hot. What a day they picked for you to wash the chickens."

"What do you mean?" he asked.

"Well," I said, "you've got to wash each chicken by dipping it in warm water and flea soap."

Benny started to unravel, "There's 500 chickens here! I can't catch and wash 500 chickens in this heat!"

I said, "I know, that's why I feel sorry for you."

Well, the joke spread like wild fire and everyone wanted to help it along. Workers came into the milk room in ones and twos and say, "Hey Benny, I hear they picked today to wash the chickens. Sorry, man."

Even Mr. Kovitch walked in, pretending not to see Benny behind him, and said to me with a straight face, "Tutt, did you tell the chicken man he has to wash the chickens today? Make sure he knows it's got to be done before lunch."

Poor Benny, he spent at least half an hour asking all his buddies if they would help him. When I finally let him off the hook, he was so relieved he couldn't get angry. I'm sure glad he was a good sport. It took our minds away from the heat for a little while.

Another inmate who resonates, even all these years later, is Doug (I guess he missed the call for nicknames). I met Doug one afternoon when I went out to sit at my flower garden, just outside the office door. He was new to the farm, a tall, quiet Black man, who was serving his second prison term. He sat next to me, introduced himself, and started a casual conversation, but I could sense something was bothering him, so I just let him talk, chipping in a word or two when prompted. Finally he came to the point.

"Mr. Tutt, I know you're different. Anyone can see it in you. And I know it's your God. Can you really talk to your God?"

He explained that he had become a Muslim during his first prison sentence, but that he sensed there was still something missing. We talked, nothing heavy; he mainly wanted to know how I could be so happy. I told him about Jesus and a few of the differences between our religions. The main difference, I said, was that his god didn't seem to love or forgive, and mine did both. He didn't say or ask much, but I could tell he was processing. Then it was time to eat, so we walked to the mess hall together. He sat next to me, but the loud table conversations made it impossible to talk further. After dinner we went our own ways, doing our own jobs.

I was waiting with some of the CIA guys that night in the common area; we were heading over to our weekly meeting. Doug came in and pulled something from the fridge, and we exchanged nods. He surveyed our little group with interest as we laughed and jostled each other on our way out the door. Not 15 minutes later, Doug came strolling into our meeting and took a seat. I almost fell off my chair. He couldn't have picked a better night. We were listening to a tape by Christian evangelist Corrie TenBoom (If you haven't read her book, *The Hiding Place*, I highly recommend you do). She talked about her time in a Nazi prison camp, where her entire family had been imprisoned for helping Jews escape the Gestapo. She and her fellow Christian prisoners praised the Lord continuously despite the harsh conditions. They even praised Him when they contracted lice because it kept the guards out of their sleeping areas, enabling them to study the Bible they'd smuggled in, and they praised Him as her sister died, knowing she would soon be truly free. After the tape Doug said, "Wow. And we think we've got it bad."

Later, Doug asked me if I could get him a Bible, which I immediately did. And guess who else asked for a Bible that night? Mario, my Italian buddy. I had to request one in Italian from the civilians who attended the CIA meetings, and they brought one the next week.

As I said earlier, those civilians impressed me. They never missed a meeting, even in the worst blizzard conditions. I decided to learn more about this man named Chuck Colson. He, too, had become a Christian just before serving his sentence. When he returned to civilian life, he made it his mission to minister to inmates by bringing the Gospel to them. I wondered if I could do something like that when I got out.

In August, my sweet Jenny began to fade as the cancer became too much for her body to handle. I asked Audrey to make sure she sent my love whenever she visited because every time I tried to write to Jenny, no words would come. What I wanted to say, I wanted to say in person. As letters from Sam became more and more dire, I prayed fervently that Jenny would accept Jesus before she died. I still didn't know if she even had the capacity to understand what that meant.

The phone call came at the end of August. It was Sam, telling me she had only days left. I requested a furlough through my chain of officials. They said I'd need an escort, and said I might rather wait and go to the funeral. I couldn't go twice.

"It won't matter at the funeral," I said. "I want to go now."

I was at the hospital the next day. My heart sank when I saw her. My 50-year-old sister looked about 100. Her hair was gray and her face pale and tired. When she saw me, though, her eyes lit up and my spirits lifted. We exchanged warm words of love and greetings. I asked the CO if I could be alone with her, and he stepped into the next room.

Certain that she could understand me, I told her Jesus loved her and died for her so that she could live, even after death, but she had to confess she was a sinner, as we all are and ask Jesus to come into her heart. I asked if she understood and she said "Yes, I want Jesus to come into my heart."

I was hours from losing my sister, yet I was overcome with joy.

Still, I wanted to be sure. I sat by her as she dozed off, and when she awoke, I asked her if she remembered what we had just talked about. She replied, "Yes, Jesus." She pointed across the room and said, "Jesus just got up off his chair and came to me."

With hindsight, I realize the Lord would have taken her to Heaven, regardless. He cares for those who can't comprehend Him, with the same wild abandon He has for the rest of us, and He is just. I think Jesus orchestrated that last moment for me, to assure me in my distress that all would be well.

Jenny died three hours later. I'm still thankful that the Lord let me see her one more time.

I returned to the Annex one week before my MPI board. It was a long week for me, and for Big John. The suspense was almost maddening as we played out all the potential scenarios. After seeing what happened to Jacko and Red, we tried not to get our hopes up. I was hoping for 18 months, the least possible minimum, which would make me eligible for parole in May.

On the morning of the board I did nothing to prepare except pray for that peace that passes all understanding, because I knew the Lord would bring about the decision that best suited His purposes and not necessarily mine. The board convened in the visiting room, where I sat before three commissioners, a stenographer, and two unidentified observers. One commissioner asked me if I was involved in any programs (enrolling in vocational programs earns an inmate points on his record). I answered that I worked 12-14 hours every day, that I was president of the CIA, teaching an English class, attending Bible classes, and helping in the mess hall, and that I had no time left for anything else. He said, "I can see why."

He asked what I intended to do when I was released. I said I planned to get a job, and that I was considering becoming involved in Prison ministry, and I briefly explained why. I started to talk about discrepancies in my arrest and trial, but he stopped me with an abrupt, "Thank you. We'll let you know our decision."

The entire meeting lasted about three minutes. That couldn't be good.

I sat outside the visitors' room for only a few minutes more. Then the door opened and the commissioner handed me their decision.

Eighteen months.

No song could have sounded sweeter at that moment.

I rushed back to write Audrey, and found Big John sitting at my doorway looking forlorn and small. He'd been hit with three years. We talked for a few moments and then he went to lie on his bed, where he stayed, looking at the ceiling, for the rest of the day. He didn't even come out that night for snacks.

The next evening he was back at my door. I don't know what had happened the night before, but I was looking at a changed man.

"I want to talk about God, Joe," he said.

"Of course!" My heart soared. We talked for nearly two hours, about love, repentance, forgiveness. He had been reading the Bible and attending CIA meetings off and on since his sister's recovery, so the concepts were not new to him, but I sensed an earnest hunger this time.

Finally, he stood up and said, "Joe, I know this is real. He is real. I know I will need Him if I'm going to make it three years here. I want to accept Jesus, but I don't know how."

I don't know when I've ever been happier. We read the four spiritual laws together, and then he prayed, even more fervently, I thought, than he had for his sister. Then, Praise the Lord, he gave his life to Christ.

For the next few weeks I watched Big John's amazing transformation in awe. I could hardly believe he was the same man who had been walking around in a daze after the MPI board, or the imposing gang leader who could make a man cower with just a look. Instead, he emanated joy and peace, and his tough-guy persona disappeared completely, which confused many of the other inmates. I heard one inmate musing as he shook his head, "I don't know what's got into him, but I gotta get some of it."

I had to laugh. Ten months earlier Big John had been saying that about me.

With my minimum sentence set at 18 months, I was now eligible to apply for a furlough and for work release. The first would give me a week home with my family, and the second would allow me to transfer to a prison where I'd be able to work in the community for minimum wage. I sent applications to Albany immediately, asking to be sent to Albion so I could work near home.

Home. Even if I didn't get the furlough or work release, having an established 18 month minimum meant that in just eight more months I *could* be home for good.

Ain't God Great!

November, 1978

I had to wait seven weeks for the furlough and work release decisions to come back from the main office in Albany. In most cases, such decisions are based on an inmate's accumulated "behavior" points: 32 for a furlough and 35 for work release. I had 37 points, the most one can obtain in the amount of time I'd served. However, because I was in a CMC status, the decision was not as simple. I prayed daily for God's favor and got on with my work.

The seemingly endless list of farm chores waiting to be done helped pass the time. Ol' Tino had impregnated many of the cows early in the summer, and others had been artificially inseminated. We would monitor them throughout the winter, ensuring they received sufficient nutrition, maintaining their vaccination schedules, watching for parasites, trimming their hooves, and just trying to keep them as comfortable as possible. I loved my ladies very much, and it was a sad realization to think I might not be around to see them give birth in the spring.

I kept up my kitchen work, too, although it was starting to look as if Crazy Stella was going to work out fine. He'd given up his cult and was now earnestly trying to follow the Bible's teachings. I'd taught him nearly everything I knew about cooking, and, although his menu was weighted rather heavily on the Italian side, the inmates seemed to like his food. I popped in at least twice a day to see if he needed my help; usually he didn't. Still, I'd grab a spoon and take a bit of whatever he had simmering and pretend to look off into my mother's kitchen (my standard for perfection) as I assessed the flavors. Crazy Stella would stare at me with hope-filled eyes, clenching the front of his apron until I brought my fingers together up to my mouth and kissed them open proclaiming, "*Exquisita!*"

We pulled up the last of the vegetables in the prison garden in September. Crazy Stella served potatoes at every meal for a month, but boy, were they good. We appreciated all the fresh food we could get, knowing winter was coming.

Every morning, the mountains were more beautiful than they'd been the day before. I never tired of making that trek up to the mess hall or back down to the dairy. We'd had a few small flurries, but nothing to equal the snow storms of the previous winter. By the end of October, all the reds and golds had fused into a rust-colored blanket that was becoming thread-bare, and I could once again see the mountains of Vermont in the distance.

Our weekly CIA attendance was at an all-time high. There seemed to be no end to our list of volunteer guest speakers and inmate testimonies, always followed by riveting, Bible-based discussions. The talks were always uplifting, and we tried as best we could to carry the sense of peace and fellowship from those meetings into our day-to-day interactions with other inmates. Big John's natural leadership abilities were evident as he encouraged others to participate in the talks and to read their Bibles back at the Annex. It tickled me to see inmates start knocking at *his* door in the evenings with their questions. I knew God was preparing me to leave this place, and that it was time for Big John to step into my role. So, in mid-October, I handed him the reins and he became the new CIA president.

One morning in early November, Mr. Kovitch pulled me out of the kitchen and said he was going hunting for a week.

"I need you to run things, Tutt," he said. "Make sure you keep the books up and keep the inmates on task. The girls need you to look out for 'em."

"What about the other COs," I asked. "Don't you think I'd be stepping on toes?"

"Those two would screw it up on their own, and they know it. You won't hear any complaints from them. They've seen how you keep this place going, and frankly, they don't *want* the extra responsibility."

I worked hard that week, and everyone pitched in to make sure all went off without a hitch. When I wrote to Audrey about it, she said it was just another way I resembled Joseph in Genesis; he went from being a prisoner to managing the pharaoh's storehouses in just a short time. I had to agree, and like Joseph, I was aware the entire time that God was the one doing the "heavy lifting," so I couldn't take credit for all that went right that week, but I was sure delighted to see that Mr. K was pleased when he returned.

On November 8, after a long day on the farm, followed by a fantastic but exhausting evening at CIA, I returned to my room to find a letter lying on my bed. My chest tightened when I saw it was from the central office in Albany. My next steps had been decided. I said a quick prayer before opening the envelope. Of course, it would have been senseless to petition God for good news at that point, so I just prayed an acknowledgement that His will in my life had served me well thus far, and pledged to accept the decision with peace and contentment.

I read only as far as the first lines before I dropped to my knees against the tidal wave of relief and gratitude that washed over me. The letter granted approval for both furlough and work release; and not only that, but it stated the work release would be at Albion. I'd been preparing myself for the worst so intently that the notice took me by surprise. Things like this just don't happen, and all I could say was, "Ain't God Great!"

Of course, this meant my life was about to change again. The prison staff would be dropping me from the Close Monitoring list because they couldn't watch me "out there." Such an occurrence was unusual, but I'd learned that God specialized in making the seemingly impossible possible. Fortunately, they said I could continue to work on the farm until I transferred.

I took my furlough the third week in November. I briefly considered delaying the visit to be home for Thanksgiving, but I didn't know how long it would be before the Work Release details would be finalized. If the transfer came too soon, it could usurp my furlough, so I thought I'd better high-tail it home before someone changed his mind.

Poor Audrey had only about a week's notice before my visit, and she had a rather ambitious list of things for me to accomplish while I was home. My eyeglasses were nearly useless, so I'd need to see the ophthalmologist (prison exams were not exactly meticulous), and although I hadn't had any dental problems I wanted to keep it that way, so she arranged a dentist appointment; and she wanted a doctor to look at my shoulder (always a nurse). I also wanted to experience a few of the things I'd taken for granted before my arrest: stand in a real store, walk down the lane, eat in a restaurant— I was even excited at the idea of checking my own mailbox.

The moment I left the prison I rushed to the airport to grab a "puddle jumper" from Plattsburg to Albany. From there I hopped on a commercial flight to Buffalo. While I was standing in line in Albany to purchase my ticket, a young man jumped right in front of me as if I weren't even there. I'd been incarcerated so long that his behavior shocked me. This sort of thing just doesn't happen in prison. You'd have five pairs of hands on your shoulders in a second and find yourself in a corner nursing some rather nasty bruises while the line resumed. I checked my temper by reminding myself just how wonderful the week ahead was going to be, and perhaps more importantly, that I was not the person I used to be, and then I stepped back to give him room.

Being home was surreal. A couple of times during that week I had a fleeting thought that I'd been on some crazy undercover assignment and was back in my real world, but little reminders would snap me quickly out of it, like when pain shot up my arm, or when I looked in the mirror and saw how much I'd changed. There was no anger in my face, only peace. I found it hard to believe I was looking at a convicted felon.

It was wonderful to see Audrey, and Joey too, who had come home for Thanksgiving break. He was so tall and mature I couldn't stop looking at him. I listened with pride as he spoke about his classes (in which he was thriving), and about attending Campus

Crusade meetings. He was on the brink of accepting Christ, I could just *see* it.

Audrey had made my medical appointments with long-time family acquaintances, none of whom charged us for their services. What a blessing that was! The doc thought he might be able to help my arm, but not during the furlough. I told him I hoped to be back for good soon and would schedule a visit at that time.

We went to dinner with Mother and Dad at a nice, lake-side restaurant, and we visited friends and family. At one point, someone said to my son, "I can't believe your father was an undercover cop. He looks more like he should have been a mailman, judging by his demeanor."

Joey said, "Yeah, well, he found God."

The highlight of my visit, however, was attending Sunday morning service at Lockport's CMA Church. I didn't know until that morning how closely the congregation had been following my story. I'd sent numerous letters, which had been typeset and copied for parishioners. When Pastor Bob offered me the floor I thought it would be an excellent opportunity to thank everyone for supporting the *Friends for Joe* program. Their outpouring of love had made it possible for Audrey to visit me seven times and bring me countless packages. As I was expressing our profound gratitude, I noticed a hand in the air and nodded to the woman in the third row.

"Has Crazy Stella learned how to cook?" she asked.

"What about Big John?" said someone else, "Do you think he needs Bibles?"

Then someone from the choir said, "I'd really like to write to Lorenzo about his son dying because that happened to me too. Do you think he'd mind?"

On and on it went. They wanted to know about everyone. They'd become drawn into the lives of Jacko, Harl, Lefty & Shorty, and so many other people I'd written to them about, to the point where some even said they felt as if they knew the inmates personally. I had tears in my eyes before we finished. I stayed long after the service to answer as many of their questions as I could, and accepted their well-wishes to bring back to the inmates. So much joy, and such a welcome. I'm still overwhelmed to think of it.

I savored every moment of that wonderful week at home. Even the nights where I just sat with Audrey and Joey watching television were great blessings. Too soon, the time came to head back. We piled into Dad's Cadillac and I drove us to Clinton. What a privilege it was to feel my hands on the steering wheel. We enjoyed the trip immensely; even though the leaves had dropped from the trees by that time, the views heading upstate were spectacular. When we reached the prison, the guards made a note that I reported back in a Caddy.

No sooner had I checked myself in than it was time to leave again, this time for good. My transfer to Albion was scheduled for December 12, 1978, giving me less than a week to train my replacements and say my good-byes. Needing some alone time, I walked up to the patch of ground that used to be my garden. The frost had obliterated every stalk and stem. Someone else would have to breathe new life into it next spring. As I sat on my wall, praying in thanksgiving for whatever the Lord had in store for me at Albion, Kuba came around the corner. It seemed like ages since I'd jumped in front of his massive fists to break up a fight, but it had only been a few months. I wouldn't exactly say we'd been friends, but we'd developed a mutual respect, of sorts.

"Hey, Tutt," he said, "Been looking for you. I'm leaving in the morning, and I wanted to say good-bye."

When I stood up to shake his hand, he surprised me with a big hug. Not the typical way one says goodbye to the man who put him behind bars.

"You're not the same guy who put me in here," he said, leaving one hand on my shoulder. "I want you to know I learned a lot from you, and I wanted to thank you."

"Well I'm sure glad," I said, "but I don't understand. We never even talked."

"Sometimes it ain't about what a man says."

Kuba flashed a pearly white smile, then turned and walked along the path toward the Annex. As I watched him leave, it occurred to me that he'd been at every CIA meeting since that week he came with Tank. He'd never said a single word in those meetings, but I imagine the Lord had been working on him the entire time. I prayed for Kuba for many weeks after that, knowing he was out there trying to assimilate into the world's culture. I knew it wasn't easy for anyone, but perhaps he had an edge, now that he knew Jesus as I suspected he did.

I wrote a letter to Mr. Licata, the pizza shop owner in Lockport, asking if he would consider letting me work at his shop for my work release. I would have understood if he'd declined but he didn't. Instead, he sent me an animated reply saying he was thrilled by the idea, and urging me to hurry back. He actually said he needed me. That sure felt good.

The time came to leave the farm, which was surprisingly difficult. I spent the week looking at every event as "the last"— my last Sunday service at Clinton, the last time chatting with my ladies, the last meal I would help prepare in the kitchen.

On the morning before I left, I was sitting on a bale of hay with Ben Vaughn, the farm's head civilian, a nice, quiet man in his late 50s. We were enjoying the early morning peace, watching Jacko and Lefty working together to push an overloaded wheel barrow into the barn. I'd gotten to know Ben much better since starting my clerking job. We'd talked about many things during quiet moments just like this one. He'd heard me refer to my faith many times, saying such things as, "If it's in the Lord's will," and, "Praise the Lord," etc., but in all our discussions we'd never talked about God. Well, I guess he sensed his last window of opportunity closing, because right out of the blue, he asked, "Tutt, do you really believe in a life hereafter?"

That was all I needed. Once again I had the advantage, and the rusty shovel. I knew Ben was coming from the same place I'd been before my arrest, shouldering all the same questions and doubts.

"I do, Ben," I said. "The greatest gift Jesus gave us was victory over death. At least, that's what it says in the Bible."

"I don't understand that thing," he said. "It's too confusing with all those parables and the symbolism. My priest tells us what it says, but it don't always help. I'm just an ordinary man."

"Well, someone once told me, and I've come to agree, that the Bible is a letter from God to each one of us. To you, too, if you've got questions. When you let others read it for you, you miss out on the joy of discovery. If you're having trouble with the language, try a different Bible. One that's straightforward and in English."

"Where do you think I might get one?"

"I can bring you one tomorrow," I said. "I've given my Bibles to Big John but he'll gladly let me have one back. You can ask him about anything that stumps you and he'll help you work through it."

I could tell by looking in his eyes that he was genuinely thirsty.

"That would be great," he said. "You won't forget, now will ya?"

"As if I could."

I praised the Lord all day long.

Saying good-bye to the inmates was particularly difficult, which is odd, considering these were thieves and murderers I was leaving behind. I went to one last CIA meeting that night. Big John looked just right in his place at the front of the room. His face glowed, and I knew he was right where the Lord wanted him to be. I clapped Jacko on the back, but neither of us could speak. Lefty, Shorty, Doug, and many whose names I've forgotten, all lined up to exchange handshakes, hugs, and thank-yous. Big John led a corporate prayer for my protection, and I joined in with praise and petition for all the men in our group. It was an emotional time, but I knew these men were going to be all right, and I left them in John's capable hands. They'd all be at work when I left in the morning.

It was hardest to say good-bye to Mr. Kovitch, and I think the feeling was mutual.

"What do you want to leave for? You've got it made here," he said.

If it weren't so far away, I would have been tempted to stay. This farm experience had been wonderful; it was everything I love to do.

"You know, I'd love to stay on," I said, "But Audrey has to drive eight hours to see me. I have a job lined up a few blocks from my home, and I'm looking forward to being closer to my family."

I asked him for his home address so I could write him, which he gave me. I waited until I'd been gone about 6 months. When I wrote, I chose my words carefully, in case it would be read. I didn't want any of his superiors to think he was giving favoritism to any of the prisoners. I remember writing, "Hey, I can call you Bill now. It felt strange calling you Mr. K when I felt like a brother." I also let him know I thought he'd been tough, but fair in his management style, and that I'd been proud to work for him. I didn't write again, as much as I wanted to. Sometimes friendships just have to end, but I'll always treasure the moments we shared and the confidence he placed in me.

I left Clinton early in the morning on December 12th, handcuffed and leg shackled to a "traveling companion." The trip to Albion would be an over-nighter because we didn't exactly drive straight to Buffalo. Instead of heading west, we took off to the south along the Hudson River, stopping at prisons in Albany and Poughkeepsie to load and drop off prisoners. We ended up at Sing Sing, almost on the Pennsylvania border, where we holed up for the night.

The guards removed our handcuffs and shackles and transferred us to individual cells. Prisoners in transit could not mingle with the Population, but that didn't guarantee the Population wouldn't mingle with the visitors. As soon as someone recognized me and yelled, "DA from Buffalo!" I knew I'd better be on my guard.

The prison grapevine is far more efficient than any other communication system known to man. In no time at all, word of my arrival spread, and the "feeders" began making their way down the corridor. Feeders were inmates who pushed a cart laden with coffee and boxed meals for those who could not leave their cells. They looked like airline stewards, stopping at each cell to let the inmates select from a pile of sandwiches and snacks, and passing the food between the bars.

They'd been looking for me. When they reached my cell, one of the feeders stopped and gave me a long, hard, loathing stare. I just stared back; I may have arrested him, but he didn't look familiar. I stayed in the shadows, and asked only for coffee.

"Looky here," he said to his buddy, "If it ain't the DA!"

Correcting him would have been pointless so I just let him go on.

He stepped closer to my cell, examining me as if I were a specimen, then lowered his voice to a growl.

"Do you know how much I hate you? You and all your law-man friends? What a stroke of luck this is, us meeting up this way. I just may have me an opportunity that I'll never get again."

We both knew I was safe as long as I didn't go near the bars or call out to the guards to open the cell door. His attention was focused on making me do just that.

"Let's see...I wonder if we could smoke you out..."

He pulled a match from his pocket and looked at the cart for something that would catch easily. His partner did nothing.

I calmly walked over to the sink and put a towel under the spigot. If I held it to my face I could out-wait him. He didn't have enough fuel on that cart to make much of a fire.

He must have decided the same thing, because he returned the unused match to his pocket and instead dangled his clipboard just inside my cell, holding it loosely between his thumb and forefinger.

"I guess I could tell the C.O. I've dropped this here roster into your cell and have to retrieve it. What do you suppose I would do when he opens it for me? You know we're going to come in and kill ya, don't you?"

His partner stood tall and looked nervously toward the guard area. I couldn't tell whether he wanted to fight, but I couldn't rule it out.

As calm as I appeared on the outside, my mind was spinning with activity.

Many times before that night I'd thought about the Israelites in the Book of Exodus, crossing the dessert. God did everything for them...provided shelter, water, food, even sandals that didn't wear out, and yet, they thanked him with whining and more demands. I used to be puzzled at how the Jews could be so foolish, after all God gave them, to keep forgetting and complaining, and to keep turning away from him. I was about to find myself in the same state of forgetfulness.

I put aside all the Lord had done for me over the past year and told myself I was on my own. My police instincts flooded through my veins like an old friend. I removed my glasses—they were still rather new after all—and devised a hasty plan. I'd already noticed the cell door opened only about 18 inches and locked automatically when it slid closed. Such a small opening meant they would have to enter one at a time. I was sure I could take each one as he entered and knock him unconscious, then I could shove their bodies to the other side of the corridor and slide the cell door shut with me safely inside.

That's when I remembered the book of Exodus, and I froze. After all the Lord had done for and through me. Pictures flashed across my mind like a movie—Chiefy, Big John, Kuba—and I realized I was doing the very same thing as the Israelites. If I believed God had a plan for my life, I had to believe whatever was about to happen was part of that plan, and that this moment wasn't a surprise to Him.

I put my glasses back on and decided to trust God. Yes, I was incredibly concerned, but I was not afraid. The next words out of my mouth took all three of us by surprise, and to this day I have no idea why I said them.

"Well, if you want to come in, go right ahead," I said. "But let me warn you, there's an angel in here with me and you'll have to contend with him first."

They looked behind me and their eyes widened; then they looked at each other and left abruptly. Simple as that. I have no idea what they saw behind me. When I turned around I saw nothing but cement wall. Whatever it was convinced them to leave me alone, and I never saw them again. I'll say it again, Ain't God great?

There were no more incidents at Sing Sing; I got a good night's sleep, and we continued our journey to Albion the next day. At the time, Albion Correctional Facility was primarily a woman's prison, with one building (Building D) set aside for men in the work release program. The building resembled a dormitory, separated from the outside world by just a fence, and with a door facing the street. Guards stood their posts at the door, where we entered or left the prison.

I was eager to start working, but it took a few days to process and settle in. I had my own room again, but there were beds for others should the need arise (later, the guards moved me to a one-bed room, which I truly appreciated.) I had little contact with the other inmates there. However, I did befriend one of the guards.

His name was McNally. He stuck his head in my door one day and blew me away with his introduction. As it turned out, he had been planning to apply for a job in Narcotics with me before my arrest. He changed his mind after what happened to me.

"I thought you were really something," he said. "I wanted to work for you."

I felt sick. At first, I thought it was such a shame; with his young features and those thick curls, he would have fit in real well as an undercover agent. Had I robbed him somehow? Or perhaps his *not* going undercover might have been God's intended plan for him. I couldn't dwell on it.

McNally was in charge of my area in the prison, so we talked often. He asked me about "this church stuff," and I told him what I knew. I even shared with him my story about Sing Sing. He was a smart kid, and I watched him process who he thought I'd been and what I'd become. I knew a seed had been planted.

Another person surprised me one afternoon by flinging my door open when I was taking a shower. He opened it with such flair that I was startled.

"Hiya, Joe! I knew if I hung around long enough I'd run into you eventually!"

It was Billy, the inmate from Attica who had wanted to pass the inmate hat for my *Friends for Joe* account. I dressed and came out to sit with him. We talked about home and the parishioners who'd been helping each of us. It was good to talk to him. We chatted quite often after that, and enjoyed each other's company.

Once I started working at Licata's, my life fell into a predictable routine. I would get up every morning, have breakfast, clear the prison gate security, walk to the highway and board a public bus to work. After I worked eight hours, someone from Licata's would drive me to the bus station and I'd return to the prison. I wasn't allowed to detour at all. The prison staff monitored my travel times closely, and searched me when I returned, taking any change I had from my bus fare, gum, hard candy, handkerchief, whatever I happened to have on me. I could bring nothing into the prison. Occasionally, they demanded a urine sample for analysis to make sure I wasn't drinking or doing drugs; it was standard procedure for a work release inmate. The situation was similar to the farm: you do what's expected because you don't want to lose the privilege.

I enjoyed working at Licata's. It was a thriving restaurant, particularly on the week-ends, but I only worked week days. Fran was very nice to me, and even let me tweak his menu a bit. I introduced spaghetti and meatball dinners, which went over pretty well. Fran and his co-owner, Charley, would get into disagreements and I occasionally found myself in the role of mediator, most likely because I was older than most of their workers.

The pizzeria was practically across the street from my house, but I did not dare risk my work release to go home. Still, it felt good to be close. Audrey could stop by, although her visits were rare because she was usually on duty in Buffalo when I worked, but it made me smile to think we were passing each other daily. She visited me at Albion on the weekends.

Another reason I didn't try to go home was that I had to walk out my Christian life before the world. I knew that I was being watched everywhere I went, by inmates, by prison officials, by the Licata staff, and by public citizens. If I cheated, it would be like giving black eyes to my fellow Christians.

The pay was great, considering my previous years' wages. At the farm, by the time I left, I was getting $1.30 per week (that was top pay; others were paid .50 cents a week). However, I received minimum wage at Licata's, which was about $5 an hour. Instead of giving it to me, they mailed it to the prison, where it was deposited into my account.

When I wasn't working, I counted the days until my parole board in May. Just about every inmate in the Work Release program was waiting for that all-important event. Boards were held monthly. I'd hear the inmates talk about them in the evenings, and most came back with the same report: "They said I could apply again in six months."

That was standard chairman lingo for, "we think you're not ready."

Two main issues could prevent a person from getting parole: black marks on his record indicating that he had a temper or was inclined to return to the same behavior that had landed him in jail, and failure to show repentance for his act. When my turn came, it was the second issue that was going to get me. I would never confess to this crime that I hadn't committed.

While I waited, I found a way to make myself useful at Albion. I was listening to McNally one afternoon lamenting that the prison had a van but nobody to drive it.

"Well, I have a still-valid Class-II license from my police days."

"You do?" McNally sat upright. "Where is it?"

I called Audrey, and she brought it that weekend.

One of the COs took me out for a test ride. He made me turn this way and that, back up, and all that. The large, 8-passenger van required some skill to drive, but I'd been well-trained in defensive driving as a police officer, so I knew my stuff.

"Hey, you could teach *me* a few things." He checked the box marked "pass."

So, I became the inmate driver, which added nearly two hours to my daily routine, but I didn't mind at all. I'd become accustomed to long days on the farm, and frankly, there wasn't a lot to do at Albion to pass the extra time. Most of the inmates had work-release jobs in Rochester, so I would drive them to the city, return the van (stop at the gate for inspection), then go back to my room and get ready for work; walk back through the gate, and then walk to the bus stop. I had to leave the van at the prison in case they needed it during the day. Every night, I'd take the bus to Albion, check in and get the van, and then drive to Rochester to get the guys. Eventually, since the van was so rarely needed, the CO relented and let me drive it to Licata's during the day, which saved a little time.

With the exception of the Big Strike, my months in Albion passed in a relatively uneventful manner. Perhaps the greatest moment of my entire prison sentence occurred on January 28, 1979, when I received a still-treasured letter from Joey:

"Dear Pops, Well, I'm back in school, and class work is going ok, but you should know, I hate it here. I miss Lockport and the people there, especially at church. They're all so nice, and it's just, well, different here. I guess I had to leave Lockport to see it. I think it really hit home when I saw you in November, and how happy

you looked. I realized this week that the difference is the folks in Lockport have Jesus.

"I've decided I want to know the Lord like you do, and Aud, and Gram and Gramps. That's why last night at the Campus Crusade meeting, I gave my life to Christ. As soon as I did, I knew it was the right thing. I sat up with friends until about 2:30 a.m. talking about God. I even told them your story and they were very impressed and want to meet you.

Well, I have to go now, but I wanted you to know. I'll write again soon with more details. Love ya, Joey."

I read and re-read the letter several times. I couldn't see it all the first few times because of the tears that kept blotting my vision. After that, all I could do was dance and holler, "Praise the Lord!" It was another example in our family that the Lord does answer prayer.

The prison strike began April 19 and lasted 16 days. It was not just at Albion, but throughout the state, where more than 6,400 correctional officers at 33 facilities refused to work to protest low pay, poor benefits, and unsafe working conditions. The governor, a man named Hugh Carey, activated around 12,000 National Guardsman to guard the prisons.

Many guards at Albion didn't strike, and were considered scabs. The strikers outside wouldn't let them out across the picket lines, so they were stuck in the prison for the duration. The work release program in Rochester was suspended, but Mr. Licata said I could continue working in his shop as long as I could get there. Surprisingly, the striking guards had no problem letting me drive the van through the picket lines.

As it turned out though, I didn't always go to work. Instead, I became the conduit between the guards and their families. The guards on the inside would call their spouses to let them know I was coming and ask for some supplies, then they'd give me directions to their homes, where I'd pick up their items. I hid packages under the seats furthest to the back of the van, which is pretty far back in an 8-

passenger vehicle. The strikers inspected the van when I returned, but never thoroughly, and they never found my "contraband."

When I did go to work, Mr. Licata was very interested in what was happening at the prison. He would read about the strike in the local papers, and then ask me about what I knew about it. I told him both sides were right, and I just hoped it would be over soon, because my parole board was coming up. One day he sent a pile of pizzas back to the prison. I dropped some boxes off with the strikers at the gate, and brought the rest inside for the guards. It made the papers that some inmate was bringing them pizza, and the public response was, "So what? Nothing unlawful about that."

The strike ended on a Friday, May 4, 1979, but I did not resume my routine. Instead, McNally poked his head in my room with an announcement.

"Hey, Tutt," he said. "You're going to have to tell your boss you won't be working Monday."

"What's up?"

"You'll be at your parole board."

As exciting as it sounded, I didn't have high hopes. I'd been running this scenario through my head every which way and always came out losing. They would ask me to admit my crime and show remorse for committing it, but I couldn't. I knew how it worked. Even people who claimed they were innocent were expected to say they were sorry. Even if it meant lying. They'd take any excuse:

I did it because I was a drug addict.

I had a screwed up childhood.

The voices in my head told me to do it.

There are a thousand excuses you could use that would satisfy the board. But I couldn't use any of them, and I wouldn't.

On Monday morning, I prepared the only way I knew how. I prayed. I put the entire matter into God's hands and vowed to accept whatever decision He made for my future. Audrey knew I was going before the board and was also praying for me with her friends from church. When the time came to report in, I felt absolute peace.

The panel consisted of three members, all wearing suits and holding black pens. They were looking over my record when I entered. The chairman looked up and motioned me to a chair.

"Please sit, Mr. Tuttolomondo," he said. "We were just reading some rather remarkable comments in your file. I must say, I'm a bit surprised; former police officers tend to get into all kinds of trouble in prison."

"I just did what I was told, Sir, and tried to help where I could."

"That's evident in the file," he said. "Tell me, you've had time now to consider the consequences of your actions. Do you feel any remorse over what you did?"

There it was. The start of my next six months. I looked the man in the eye and told him I could not answer that question.

"Even though I know I'll get more time," I said, "I cannot admit to a crime I did not commit. But I will say this: If I could go back in time and turn the tables on those who did this to me and lose what I've got now, I'd never do it."

They looked surprised, and started whispering among themselves. The discussion was brief, but it seemed like hours to me. I prepared myself for that stock answer: *"Perhaps you should wait six months and try again."*

At last, the chairman finally looked at me and said, "Mr. Tuttolomondo, we're recommending you for immediate release."

I was so shocked I just sat there, dumbfounded until he said, "You can leave the room now."

I stood and said, "Praise the Lord!" as loudly as I dared. I walked back to my room in a daze, praising the Lord with every step, because I knew that such a decision could not have happened unless God had intervened.

Two days later I walked out the Albion gate for the last time, shaking hands with the guards. During the strike, all the nice suits in inventory that were usually given to departing inmates had somehow disappeared; all they had left in my size was an old fashioned leisure suit, which I wore proudly. I would have gone out in my underwear if I had to.

Audrey picked me up and we drove to Lockport. All the way back I could only praise the Lord and soak in the freedom of it all. The trees looked greener than I remembered them, the sky was much bluer, and Audrey was just so beautiful, I couldn't believe my good fortune. I thought about all that had happened in such a short while, and I felt only gratitude. I meant what I'd said to the parole board. I wouldn't trade a minute of it. I had no idea what the Lord was going to have me do next, but I knew I could trust Him.

We entered the driveway at our house, where a large, home-made banner had been strung across the garage door. Two of Audrey's friends had been busy while she was away; I didn't know it at the time, but every room inside was decorated with streamers and welcome signs. But for just that moment I was content to sit there, staring at the banner, tears welling in my eyes for the pure joy expressed in those three simple words:

"Home, Sweet Home."

Epilogue

*"I will restore to you the years that the
swarming locust has eaten." -- Joel 2:25*

So, how does my story end? Well, that remains to be seen, as Audrey and I are alive and well in Naples, Florida and we're as in love with the Lord as ever. But there are some loose ends to the prison story that I should probably tie up.

My transition from prison life to whatever normal would turn out to be took a bit of adjustment. For a few days the only question on my mind was, "Now what?" I'd lost so much—use of my arm, my pension, my career. I didn't know where to start getting my life back together.

Of course, I needn't have wondered. The Lord brought everything we'd lost right back to us and then some.

Almost immediately I went to the doctor, who performed surgery on my arm. It will never be completely right, but the pain went away and I regained most of my movement.

And although I worried about who would want to hire an ex-con, *that* question was resolved as well. I initially went back to work at Licata's. I figured as long as the Lord had me there, I'd be the best pizza worker I could be, and I was. I rose quickly to manager, but it took a bit of firm insistence to convince them that I wouldn't work for the minimum wage they'd paid me before. Perhaps I should have mentioned that they were quite frugal.

So yes, I was making *some* money, but even with a manager's salary we were so deep in the red that I wasn't sure how I was going to get out. I'd not given much thought to the loss of my pension while I was in prison, but now it began to grate on me. I'd had 10 years vested in the retirement system before my arrest. In the middle of my pity party, I had the audacity to think God didn't care about that. I didn't know it at the time, but there was actually a two-year time limit during which, by state law, my retirement status remained in limbo. I learned about that after left Licata's to take a job with the town of Lockport that operated under the same retirement system as the police force. When the clerk entered my name as an employee, she told me my status was active for five more days! By accepting that job, I received every bit of my retirement investiture back.

I met with a parole officer every other week for six months. He was required to see me, but there was little to talk about since I'd resumed a regular life, so I kept him abreast of my work, and we'd talk current events. We got to be friends, and I suspect he missed our talks on occasion…one day he called me on the phone and said, "Joe, where are you?"

I said, "You called me at home, where would I be?"

He had the wrong week; I still offered to come in and chat, but he turned me down.

After my release I ran into many law enforcement officers who had known me prior to my arrest. They couldn't believe the difference in me, but they couldn't accept it, either. It still makes me chuckle to remember them saying, "Joe, you're out of prison now, you can quit the religious act."

Joey excelled at the University of Wisconsin, and made the Dean's list a couple of years in a row. When he was nearing graduation, he wrote to me of his plan to apply to the Secret Service or the FBI for jobs, but I talked him out of it. Today he is married and runs a successful business (as vice president and general manager). He credits the Lord for all his accomplishments.

My daughter, Linda, is doing well also, and she gave herself to the Lord soon after I came home, filling my heart with great joy! After that, my grandchildren, all four of them became believers. I feel nothing but thanksgiving to those who had me arrested and for what followed.

As for some of the other people God placed in my life:

Leo Carlone, the attorney for the Depew boys, drowned in a swimming accident in Canada soon after I was released. I was still on parole at the time, and the accident occurred in the presence of hundreds of people at a public beach, so no one could have thought I was involved in any way. I was later told that Carlone was high on cocaine when he jumped into the water, which no doubt contributed to his death. I remembered how intent I'd been on exacting revenge, but when I heard the news, all I thought was, "Vengeance is mine sayeth the Lord." I was also somewhat sad that I'd never be able to tell him about Jesus.

About eight months after my release, I met the judge. I was sitting in a restaurant and saw him walking toward my table.

"Hi judge," I said.

He stopped and looked at me. I said, "You probably don't recognize me."

"Yes, I do." He glanced nervously about the restaurant. I do believe he was afraid I was going to start something.

I stood and shook his hand. "I just wanted you to know that I forgive you. If I had heard all that you heard, I would have thought I was guilty as well."

I could tell he was still worried, so I turned away. I didn't want to cause him any angst.

Jonathan and I corresponded while I was in prison, and one of his people came to visit me. We continued our friendship long after I came home. After Jonathan retired, he and his wife were killed in a car accident. They were good people, and I was saddened to hear about their passing.

The Conleys continue to raise support for needy causes in their community. Most recently they raised money and volunteers to facilitate a bone marrow transplant for a child who attends their church. We stay in touch and visit on occasion.

Joe Ruggiero retired from his job at University of Buffalo as Security Chief. We are still great friends today. He and his wife visit us every year.

I did hear from Lee Cupola, 35 years after my arrest. I read a story about him in the Buffalo Evening news; by then he was a professor. I sent a note to the newspaper in care of the reporter. I'd started with, "You probably won't remember me but..." I told him what had happened to me and thanked him for writing about my conversion to Christianity. I wrote, "Now, 35 years later, I want to thank you for getting the truth out. It had a profound effect on me and my family, the mere fact that the truth got out."

The reporter obviously got my note to Lee, because he wrote back. "Of course I remember you! What do you mean I won't remember?"

He thanked me for the letter and said he was glad things had worked out. I'll always be amazed at the way God worked in that situation, and in him.

I never wrote to Bill after that first letter. I worried he might get in trouble for corresponding with an inmate. I don't know how long he stayed at Clinton. A major fire destroyed the dairy farm in 2002. Responders had trouble fighting the fire because it sat in a field in the middle of nowhere, where hoses couldn't reach. That, and the fact that it was filled with hay pretty much meant the end. The damage was so extensive that the barn will not likely be replaced on the prison grounds because of the considerable cost involved.

I often think of and wonder about all the inmates I met in prison. I never had the opportunity to contact them after I left—there would have been too much involved in corresponding with an inmate (with good reason, I suppose, considering the potential for plans to be hatched). I can't help but feel that some of them, or perhaps all of them, are living spiritual and productive lives. One day I will know for sure.

After I left the prison, I felt like I'd left a mission field. I'd enjoyed talking to inmates, particularly to those who were mired in the "why me" of their incarceration, and I believed I gave them hope. I accepted many invitations to tell my story in churches and before all types of audiences. My primary goal has always been to encourage people to live without fear and to trust in the Lord's plan for their lives.

I stayed in New York long enough to secure my retirement, and then Audrey and I moved to Arizona to be closer to Joey and his family. In Arizona I received an opportunity to volunteer with Chuck Colson's Prison Fellowship and I jumped at it. I drove to the state prison every week to attend CIA meetings. At first they couldn't understand why a former Narc would travel so far to spend time with hardened criminals. They later understood I was living out the love the Lord had shown me during my own incarceration by paying it forward. I never missed a week, regardless of weather, sickness, or the occasional dust storm. Sometimes my two companions wouldn't be able to make it, but I remembered how much I'd looked forward to the CIA meetings when I'd been at Clinton, and how the civilians never let us down, and I vowed to do the same for "my" inmates. I had the privilege to do this for seven years. It was rewarding work, and we came away with so much more than we felt we offered the inmates.

Today, Audrey and I are retired and living in Naples, where we attend the First Baptist Church. My pastor, Dr. Hayes Wicker, is a gifted man who turned a piece of orange grove into a thriving, multicultural campus with some 8,000 members and an accredited Christian academy.

For many years we served in our church's child care ministry, watching 4- and 5-year-olds while their parents attended various events. As an interesting side note, when we applied for the child care position, the church conducted a background investigation that surprised us all. The investigation turned up a falsified record from October 1975 indicating that I'd been charged with possession of dangerous drugs and two counts of grand larceny. I'll never know how that report ended up in the New York records, and I was unable to get it expunged. The incident drove home for me the lengths to which someone had been willing to go just to tarnish my name. Fortunately, the church believed my version of the story (I had substantial documentation, which helped) and they opened their doors to me.

Eventually, our energy wore out and we turned over the childcare reins to a younger crew. Today we are still quite active in the church's social committee, Bible group, and Operation Christmas Child (a shoebox ministry for impoverished children in foreign lands). I also still usher during the Sunday services. What a joy it is to serve!

Over the years, I've learned that the whole world is a mission field, filled with people who don't know how awesome God is, and I've tried to live my life with a mission mindset. I'll talk to anyone about Jesus. Sometimes, though, when I'd give a testimony to a Christian group, I'd catch myself wondering whether I was just providing entertainment, or if I could truly inspire others by relating the experience of being saved. But then I'd remind myself that if just one person hears me and does something about it, it's worth everything. In the same way, if just one person reads this story and decides to learn more about the Lord, I will be overjoyed.

For those of you thinking my story didn't have as much drama as you expected it to, that's precisely why it's so powerful. Consider all that should typically happen to an ex-narcotics officer in my situation. Should I have found peace in the dark, cold basement of Clinton Prison? Should Chiefy have walked right past me without exacting punishment for his imprisonment? Should powerful gang leaders have accepted me into their fold? Absolutely not!

In the Bible story of Joseph, after he saved the Israelites from certain famine, Joseph told his brothers who had tried to kill him years earlier, "What you meant for Evil, God used for good." That's the same thing I see as I look back. Going to prison was the greatest thing that could have happened in my life, aside from marrying Audrey. When I think of it, I also know I never would have made it through this ordeal if I *hadn't* married Audrey, whose steadfast faith established the foundation that eventually saved my life. I praise God for her. But I also know that Jesus went into that cell with me, and He alone ensured I would not only survive, but thrive.

I leave you with one final thought. Freedom is foremost in life, but it's important to know what freedom is before claiming to have it. This hit home with me one day while I was talking to someone about Albion and my situation. He actually said, "Well, you really had it made there."

I told him to picture himself sitting in the best room of the best hotel imaginable, where he could order anything he wanted—food, clothing, diamonds, gold, anything. The only catch was he had to stay in the room; if he tried to leave he would be shot.

I asked him, "Would you want that?"

"Oh, no Sir," he said.

I looked him straight in the eye. "That's what freedom's all about. I was in prison for a lot more than 18 months. But I was truly free before I walked into Attica, and I'm truly free now."

I was arrested, tried and convicted and sentenced to prison for a crime I didn't commit. I used to dwell on the fact that I was innocent, but you know, it never mattered whether I committed the crime or not. What was and is important is that I turned to Jesus, the only one who could have brought me through this, not only unscathed, but with a better life than I'd had before. The Lord I once thought I didn't need turned all this mess into the most joyous event of my life and gave me a "peace that passes all understanding."

You can have that same peace.

I believe that if, after you read this book you forget who I am, you will have lost nothing, but if you forget Jesus and His forgiving grace, you will have lost everything. Yes, He's watching you, not with scorn, but with delight. To him, you are more important than the smallest sparrow, which he loves immensely. He does not care what you've done, He only cares that you are His.

His Eye is on the Sparrow

Why should I feel discouraged,
why should the shadows come,
Why should my heart be lonely,
and long for heav'n and home,
When Jesus is my portion?
My constant Friend is He:

His eye is on the sparrow, and I know He watches me;
His eye is on the sparrow, and I know He watches me.
I sing because I'm happy,
I sing because I'm free,
For His eye is on the sparrow, and I know He watches me.
"Let not your heart be troubled,"
His tender word I hear,
And resting on His goodness,
I lose my doubts and fears;
Though by the path He leadeth,
but one step I may see;

His eye is on the sparrow, and I know He watches me;
His eye is on the sparrow, and I know He watches me.
Whenever I am tempted,
whenever clouds arise,
When songs give place to sighing,
when hope within me dies,
I draw the closer to Him,
from care He sets me free;

His eye is on the sparrow, and I know He watches me;
His eye is on the sparrow, and I know He watches me.

His Eye Is on the Sparrow (Public Domain),1905;
Written by Civilia Martin; Music by Charles H. Gabriel

The Four Spiritual Laws

1. God loves you and offers a wonderful plan for your life. (John 3:16, John 10:10)

2. Man is sinful and separated from God. In that state, he cannot know and experience God's love and plan for his life. (Romans 3:23, Romans 6:23)

3. Jesus Christ is God's only provision for man's sin. (Romans 5:8, I Corinthians 15:3-6, John 14:6)

4. We must individually receive Jesus Christ as Savior and Lord. Through Him we can know and experience God's love and plan for our lives. (John 1:12, Ephesians 2:8,9, John 3:1-8, Revelation 3:20)

There is no right or wrong way to pray. God listens to your heart, not your words. However, if anyone wants to accept Jesus, one place to start is by reciting the following prayer. Look for further assistance at a church in your neighborhood. If the first one doesn't feel right, pray that God will help you and keep looking. He will, I promise.

God, I know that I am a sinner, and I am deeply sorry. I know that I deserve the consequences of my sin. However, I am trusting in Jesus Christ as my Savior. I believe that His death and resurrection provided for my forgiveness. I trust in Jesus and Jesus alone as my personal Lord and Savior. Thank you Lord, for saving me and forgiving me! Amen

About the Author

Joseph Tuttolomondo lives with his wife, Audrey, in Naples, Florida. The couple have four grandchildren: a recent college graduate embarking on a civil engineering career, a teacher of mentally challenged children; a senior in college; and a recent high school graduate. As a result of events depicted in this story, they and their parents all know the Lord for who He is.

About the Writer

Rosemarie Fitzsimmons is a Rhode Island native and retired U.S. Marine Corps gunnery sergeant. She is The Portrait Writer, a freelance writer who tells stories of courageous and positive people, particularly about God's touch on the lives of every-day heroes. Rosemarie lives with her husband, Jerry, in northern Virginia. They have two sons, Jerry and Charles and a slightly unstable Egyptian Mau named Aslan. To learn more, visit her blog at http://rosethestoryteller.com.

Joseph Tuttolomondo

Made in the USA
Middletown, DE
09 May 2016